DEFYING FATE
DÉFIER LE DESTIN

Other poetry translations by Christopher Pilling

These Jaundiced Loves (translation of
Tristan Corbière's *Les Amours Jaunes*), 1995
SUNDAY TELEGRAPH & BBC WORLD SERVICE BOOK OF THE YEAR
The Dice Cup (translation, with David Kennedy, of
Max Jacob's *Le Cornet à Dés I*), 2000
SHORTLISTED FOR THE WEIDENFELD TRANSLATION PRIZE, 2001
Love at the Full (translation of
Lucien Becker's *Plein Amour*), 2004
POETRY BOOK SOCIETY RECOMMENDED TRANSLATION, 2004
& SHORTLISTED FOR THE CORNELIU M POPESCU PRIZE
FOR EUROPEAN POETRY TRANSLATION, 2005

Maurice Carême
DEFYING FATE
DÉFIER LE DESTIN

Translated by
CHRISTOPHER PILLING

Introduced by
MARTIN SORRELL

Published by Arc Publications,
Nanholme Mill, Shaw Wood Road
Todmorden OL14 6DA, UK
www.arcpublications.co.uk

Copyright © Estate of Maurice Carême, 2009
Translation copyright © Christopher Pilling, 2009
Introduction copyright © Martin Sorrell, 2009

Design by Tony Ward
Printed in Great Britain by the MPG Books Group,
Bodmin and King's Lynn

978 1904614 48 7
978 1904614 97 5

ACKNOWLEDGEMENTS
A selection of these translations was a runner-up for the John Dryden Translation Prize 2002, sponsored by the British Comparative Literature Association and the British Centre for Literary Translation. Other poems have appeared in *Acumen*, *Other Poetry* and *Stand* and thanks are due to their editors.

The cover painting, 'Pawns in the Game', is by Geoff Morten.

The publishers acknowledge financial assistance from
ACE Yorkshire

**Arc Publications: 'Visible Poets' series
Editor: Jean Boase-Beier**

*for Sylvia
with love*

Contents

Translator's preface / 10
Introduction / 14

20 / Le cœur pur •	The pure in heart / 21
20 / Il avait du ciel •	He had sky / 21
22 / L'homme •	The man / 23
22 / Il voulut dire… •	He wanted to say… / 23
24 / La liberté •	Freedom / 25
26 / Le cri de la grive •	The cry of the thrush / 27
26 / Les illusions •	The illusions / 27
28 / Il parlait pour tuer le temps •	He talked to kill time / 29
28 / La même allée •	The same way / 29
30 / La bannière •	The banner / 31
32 / L'incrédule •	The non-believer / 33
32 / On s'habitue à tout •	You can get used to owt / 33
34 / La rue déserte •	The empty street / 35
36 / Dieu et le diable •	God and the Devil / 37
38 / Ce rien de ciel •	This dab of sky / 39
38 / La maison •	The house / 39
40 / Les navires •	Certain ships / 41
42 / Les chaînes •	Chains / 43
40 / Le peuplier •	The poplar / 41
44 / La tête •	In the head / 45
46 / Que cherchait-il… •	What was he looking for… / 47
46 / La voix •	The voice / 47
48 / Le monde est beau •	The world is beautiful / 49
50 / L'indigent •	The pauper / 51
50 / Le suicide •	The suicide / 51
52 / Les deux gamins •	The two strapping lads / 53
52 / Le misanthrope •	The misanthropist / 53
54 / Sous le ciel noir •	Under the threatening sky / 55
54 / Le mort et l'enfant •	The dead man and the child / 55
56 / La marche d'escalier •	One in a flight / 57
58 / La charrette arrêtée •	The cart's held up / 59
58 / Devant l'hôtel •	Outside the hotel / 59
60 / Il riait •	He laughed / 61

62 / Que cherchait-il?	What was he seeking? / 63
62 / La mort de Marie	The death of Marie / 63
64 / Son meilleur ami	His best friend / 65
66 / Le collectionneur	The collector / 67
66 / Il se sentit devenir…	He felt himself becoming… / 67
68 / Le chasseur	The huntsman / 69
68 / Je ne sais pas si Dieu	I don't know whether God / 69
70 / Le soir tombait	Night was falling / 71
72 / La reine morte	The dead queen / 73
72 / Le sculpteur	The sculptor / 73
74 / Le portrait	The portrait / 75
74 / L'indécis	The haverer / 75
76 / La voûte des cieux	The heavenly vault / 77
78 / Sur le quai	On the quay / 79
78 / Les cimetières	Cemeteries / 79
80 / A quoi bon s'en faire!	What's the good of worrying! / 81
80 / La fermière	The farmer's wife / 81
82 / Il avait…	What he had / 83
84 / On le laissait dire	They let him say it / 85
84 / Le mot	The word / 85
86 / Il se souvint	He remembered / 87
86 / L'envie	The desire / 87
88 / Il se dépêchait de rire	He was quick to laugh / 89
88 / Il se demanda pourquoi	He wondered why / 89
90 / Au cadran de l'éternité	On eternity's clockface / 91
90 / Avec les yeux du cœur	With the eyes of his heart / 91
92 / Celui qu'il attendait	The one he was waiting for / 93
94 / L'écrivain	The writer / 95
94 / Rien dans les mains	With nothing in his hands / 95
96 / Mélanie	Melanie / 97
96 / Le squelette	The skeleton / 97
98 / Les cieux	The heavens / 99
100 / L'angoissé	Man in anguish / 101
100 / La troupe d'anges	The band of angels / 101
102 / L'aube	Dawn / 103
104 / Baptiste	Baptiste / 105
104 / Le tiroir	The drawer / 105
106 / Le mur blanc	The white wall / 107

106 / Vous moquez-vous? •	You pulling my leg? / 107
108 / On disait •	What they said / 109
110 / Faut-il s'étonner? •	Should we be surprised? / 111
110 / Il ne parlait que du ciel •	All he talked of… / 111
112 / Il mit son coeur •	He put his heart / 113
114 / Il se revoyait •	He saw himself / 115
114 / Le canot •	The rowing boat / 115
116 / Le voyageur •	The traveller / 117
118 / Le débonnaire •	Seeing the good / 119
118 / Il s'assit •	He sat / 119
120 / Le mendiant •	The beggar / 121
122 / A force de le répéter •	By dint of repeating it / 123
124 / Il disait oui •	He said yes / 125
124 / Regardez… •	Look… / 125
126 / Les choses •	Things / 127
126 / Dans la nuit •	In the night / 127
128 / Il avait eu beau… •	In vain… / 129
128 / La faim •	Hunger / 129
130 / Que toute une allée… •	That a whole line… / 131
132 / L'affamé •	The hungry man / 133
132 / Ce petit rien •	A little something / 133
134 / L'homme et la mort •	The man and death / 135
134 / L'innocent du village •	The village innocent / 135
136 / L'artiste •	The artist / 137
136 / Il aimait caresser •	He loved stroking / 137
138 / C'était si simple •	It was so simple / 139
138 / Le tas de cendress •	The pile of ash / 139
140 / Il chercha Dieu •	He searched for God / 141
142 / L'animal •	The animal / 143
142 / Ils réclamaient •	They were appealing / 143
144 / Il viendra •	He will come / 145

Biographical notes / 147

Series Editor's Note

The 'Visible Poets' series was established in 2000, and set out to challenge the view that translated poetry could or should be read without regard to the process of translation it had undergone. Since then, things have moved on. Today there is more translated poetry available and more debate on its nature, its status, and its relation to its original. We know that translated poetry is neither English poetry that has mysteriously arisen from a hidden foreign source, nor is it foreign poetry that has silently rewritten itself in English. We are more aware that translation lies at the heart of all our cultural exchange; without it, we must remain artistically and intellectually insular.

One of the aims of the series was, and still is, to enrich our poetry with the very best work that has appeared elsewhere in the world. And the poetry-reading public is now more aware than it was at the start of this century that translation cannot simply be done by anyone with two languages. The translation of poetry is a creative act, and translated poetry stands or falls on the strength of the poet-translator's art. For this reason 'Visible Poets' publishes only the work of the best translators, and gives each of them space, in a Preface, to talk about the trials and pleasures of their work.

From the start, 'Visible Poets' books have been bilingual. Many readers will not speak the languages of the original poetry but they, too, are invited to compare the look and shape of the English poems with the originals. Those who can are encouraged to read both. Translation and original are presented side-by-side because translations do not displace the originals; they shed new light on them and are in turn themselves illuminated by the presence of their source poems. By drawing the readers' attention to the act of translation itself, it is the aim of these books to make the work of both the original poets and their translators more visible.

Jean Boase-Beier

Translator's Preface

Maurice Carême had slumbered on one of my shelves for years – apart from one or two brief wakings – since I bought him for half a crown a long way from Paris or Brussels. He was no. 128 (Editions Pierre Seghers, 1965) in *Poètes d'aujourd'hui*, a very impressive series of monographs each with a selection of poems, that I had begun to collect during my shoestring wanderings round the Latin quarter and past the *bouquinistes* along the Seine. I knew him as very readable, perhaps a little too wide-eyed and sometimes too good to be true. Seeing his name on *Défier le destin* in a bookshop in Arles in 1996 I remembered him positively enough to reach for him. With faint foreboding though, for *Défier le destin* seemed to suggest an epic struggle, and I didn't feel up to such an enterprise, even with the poet doing the hard work for me. But I discovered short poems in everyday language (apart from an odd unusual word like *pavement* and *pâquis*) and many with an unexpected switch of the tail. What's more, they were musical – of course, that's why they'd been so readable. And most had something to say that mattered. What better ways to defy fate? If you wrap up your message in obscure and discordant language who's going to bother? Many of the poems use rhyme, but are not floored by set patterns – they keep to the line of thought. Carême finds something special in mundane events or lack of events and portrays a variety of ordinary folk and their idiosyncrasies. He makes occasional entertaining excursions into the surreal and is often wondering (a favourite verb) about consequences. In context both of these work well. So does his taking God to task.

My enthusiasm for *Défier le destin* has made me realise that wide-eyed can be a virtue, for, here in this collection, the poet is not constrained by conventional or religious ways of seeing, is able to think at a tangent, is not averse to moving into fantasy but can still allow that humane values are viable. As for too good to be true, we are frequently shown the underbelly when death and pointlessness try to roll us onto our backs. A wry turn of phrase can right things unless innocence has been squashed out.

What I didn't know until recently was that Maurice Carême is considered to be one of Belgium's finest poets for children and, along with Emile Verhaeren, hailed as one of Belgium's master poets. Poems of his were set by Poulenc and Milhaud and have been translated into many languages to feature in school anthologies. Not only is there a very lively Amis de Maurice Carême – a fifty-fourth bulletin came out in September 2008 – but also a Musée Maurice Carême, where he lived in Anderlecht, and where the Fondation Maurice Carême was set up by the poet in 1975. *Défier le destin* was a posthumous work, and, like his other poems, accessible to anyone of any age.

Maurice Carême was born in 1899. In his early twenties the difficult and the obscure were in vogue, but luckily, like Lucien Becker, he changed course and aimed for child-like clarity, however dark the message. He described his aims in this way: "I try to find a form that's so stripped down that it becomes transparent enough to resemble a window through which you can see my heart beating" and added elsewhere, more sombrely: "I believe more in the heart's dark shadow than the light of intelligence". These sentiments might have led to sentimentality, but, as if aware of this possibility, he is careful to go for brevity, formality and argument along with the simple, the song-like and moving qualities he is after. But he does want to retain "enough mystery for the magic in poems not to be sacrificed".

I have a penchant for poets who rhyme or I should say who use rhyme effectively, but the corollary is that I will often consider that an adequate translation of a rhyming poem needs to be a rhyming poem. Certain liberties may have to be taken. Note my use of the passive voice here, as though an external obligation can't be gainsaid. A few examples of such challenges will give an idea of where I have been led.

In 'La marche d'escalier' (pp. 56-7) my steps need to be solid enough to withstand an extra boot, so one appears and when I want to show up the frailty of human promises an ironical "in earnest" raises its head. The poem starts with rhyming couplets – apt for steps – then there's overlap as a rhyme hops from one step to the next. That's Carême. To match this my first unrhymed verse (verse 5) has a line ending which proves to be the springboard rhyme for a leap from verse five to the final riser.

At school we were warned about *faux amis*: *éventuel* is not 'eventual', *large* isn't 'large'. And *étable* is never 'stable'. And yet it demands to be in 'La troupe d'anges' (pp. 100-1) to rhyme with table, and stable is closer than cowshed (though neither is mentioned in the gospels) to a traditional Christian birthplace with attendant angels. Since cowshed wouldn't rhyme and the presence of cows would distract, I choose 'stable' since the message of the poem is the ubiquity of angels until you start praying to hear them better.

I can even justify pulling out a plum and substituting another fruit altogether as the rhyme, not that that's the sole reason. It is in 'Mélanie' (pp. 96-7) and I change the verb too for alliterative reasons. Melanie's legs may have given up the ghost but she is so good at bringing the miracle of happiness that I'm sure she'd forgive my wordplay.

I sense that humorous touches in English often depend more on tone than in French, so there may be a tendency to tip over into the too colloquial. In the sonnet 'Dieu et le diable' (pp. 36-7), "He asked God questions" becomes "[He'd ask] God to give him the nod." At one point God insists on being at the end of a line and needs a rhyme. Of the dozen or so possibilities very few are suitable! In this same poem it is possible to balance the choice of 'heaven' rather than 'sky' for *cieux* by making hell not just blue but sky-blue! This time the comedy is not threatened by such a slight change of register.

Apart from rhyming ones there are plenty of tricky moments. In 'Vous moquez-vous?' (pp. 106-7), for example, I quite blithely translated *lumière* as 'light' until it dawned on me that light didn't seem to belong in the sequence sea-boat-light-sailor-shingle-wind-beach, so I wondered whether there was a meaning of *lumière* that I was unaware of and, sure enough, there's limber-hole – limber-holes on either side of a boat's inner keel are for drainage. A pity to lose 'light' maybe, but not when the gain in sense is as telling as here.

I see 'Il avait…' (pp. 82-3) as a sort of calling card, that is a card announcing his calling as a poet, so I don't feel too guilty about making the 'fawn' (*faon*) a fallow deer, so 'fallow' can hint at land ready for a future crop. The thrushes of his poems are their music, the fawn their youthfulness, the heavens their freedom of the air, almost a spiritual dimension. And then there's his facing up to death which I've transported from woodland to a Cumbrian 'fell' where the Mountain Rescue may need to be called. Not that I spell this out.

If I have added here what is not in the French, elsewhere I have had to subtract. In the case of 'On s'habitue à tout' (pp. 32-3) I omit the brothers' employer's job and the sister's boss's profession. We are not actually told that his brothers packed the plums. For me the ballad style adopted requires such pruning. And the narrative sounds better with packing repeated. For greater realism the mother actually speaks. I want a more simple childlike style in the last verse, so I have 'kill' for *mitrailler* (to machine-gun) and even an inversion in line two for an impression of folk-song-cum-nursery-rhyme. Again for ballad reasons I decide to keep the a-b-a-b rhyme scheme right through, though Carême doesn't, and take the liberty of changing the order of the lines in verse one. After getting us to smile at the mad ideas in this verse, the author makes the last verse seem normal and acceptable – another reason for having a narrative poem in an undeviating verse form.

To say that I have aimed for translations that are as close to the originals as possible might, after these revelations, seem preposterous but it is true. True, I hope, to the vitality of the originals. Rhymes should be unobtrusive unless their point is jocular or they go for the jugular. Not to rhyme a rhymed poem is not a crime but, where the effort to find rhymes is successful I'm walking on air. If there's a key word, say *mort*, that insists on being at the line-end, might as well throw in the towel, for there's not much you can do with 'death' if 'breath' is impossible. Then there are the poems I haven't managed to rhyme or have chosen not to. Having a bilingual edition you can judge for yourselves.

> Where Carême doesn't rhyme or does so only partially,
> Either I leave him at ease or treat him quite martially!

Christopher Pilling

Introduction

> "Poetry that is at once extremely simple, extremely lyrical, and extremely moving – and mysterious enough to maintain poetry's magic. With all my heart, I hope that some day I'll write the poem which resembles the one I've dreamt of from the day I began to write."

The words of Maurice Carême himself, in the fullest résumé I've encountered of his poetic credo. The ambition expressed is both limpid and dense, and anywhere you choose to dip into his extensive body of work – he was possessed of remarkable facility, with over two dozen collections of poems to his name, as well as an amount of prose writing – at least one of those three qualities is apparent. Simplicity. (I'm not too sure about the others, but then he's declaring an ambition, not a result). Carême's poems, pretty well all of them, including the hundred and two of *Défier le destin*, are marked by their fluency and ease of access. Here is a poetry that charms at first sight, which gives that sense of pleasure which Christopher Pilling implies in his Preface. The poems are short, seductive to the eye and ear, satisfyingly metrical and given to rhyme. Their subject matter is such as generally we recognise, and is argued and developed in ways we can follow with sympathy. Poetry to identify with, poetry of shared emotion and aesthetic satisfaction. Never does Carême seek to show off. He is an accomplished but not a complicated technician. Nor, for all that his early flirtation with surrealism and modernism has left its slight trace, is he an experimenter. One of his virtues is his sense of measure, his recognition of his boundaries; he appears wholly without envy of the gifts he does not have. For at an early stage, he found his poetic voice, and listened faithfully to it thereafter; he never needed to retrain or modulate it. An important aspect of this establishment of voice was the discovery that he had a marked talent for children's writing. Many of his publications are for children.

What Carême does in his poetry for grown ups, as does Prévert notably, and, I'd say, one or two other French poets, such as Verlaine, Fort, Fombeure, and recently Jo-Ann Léon, is to evoke and expand our shared experiences and emotions. Which he does by laying out with immediacy and a certain urgency his recurrent thoughts, joys, anxieties, moods. In a succession of miniatures, Carême captures a new, or sudden, or changing feeling or thought. Or he captures a sudden change of mood. An affective world where we all live. To an extent a confessional poet, Carême has an intuitive understanding of the person Robert Graves called the plain reader.

But if this sounds all too cosy, Carême is not as comfortable or simple as he might seem. As with the likes of Verlaine, Prévert and Léon, first impressions can be deceptive. In the matter of Carême's style – leaving aside for the moment his subject matter – all may appear simplicity itself, but technically, it's generally more sophisticated than that. Take rhyme. To achieve easy rather than facile rhyme is a sophisticated business. Especially if the trap of unintentional comic effect is to be avoided. But the rewards can be marvellous. I'm thinking particularly of Verlaine's exquisite 'Chanson d'automne', as evanescent yet substantial a set of rhymes as could be imagined, a superlative example of the art that hides art. We have deftness of the rhymester's touch in *Défier le destin*, both in the originals and these translations. Consider, say, 'The dead queen' (pp. 72-3). The original comprises a well-balanced, unobtrusive pattern of rhyme and assonance. With judicious ear and eye, Pilling has given us an equivalent pattern of his own, but one that still properly renders Carême's, respectful but not slavish. We note that 'tower' in line 1 is picked up by 'hour', line 6; 'died', line 2, is rhymed with 'wide', line 4, re-asserted in 'surprised', line 10, and given an assonantal echo in the final line; 'screech' in line 3 yields assonance with 'complete', line 7, while 'landing', line 9, rhymes with 'clanging', two lines later. Only 'stair' in line 5 stands alone, though by virtue of its final *r* it attaches itself loosely to lines 1 and 6.

A bonus of examining 'The dead queen' is that it also constitutes an excellent pointer to the insistent theme I find running through the collection, which, were I wanting to define it by a single word, I'd call anxiety. In a very substantial number of the poems of *Défier le destin*, whatever ostensibly their subject, we are in the presence of a troubled consciousness grappling with a world to which God does not deliver His reassurance. Not necessarily justice, meaning, truth – though I'd list all of these in any inventory of Carême's repertoire. What I mean is reassurance, consolation. I implied earlier that though his style might appear simple, the same is not necessarily true of his subject matter. In musical parlance, the pleasures of his accessible style and prosodic technique stand in counterpoint to the troubled nature of his argument. As if the right hand were playing bright notes while the left struck dark chords in the piano's lower registers. There's no doubt that a number of the pieces in *Défier le destin* are bright, sunlit delights. Take just one, 'The haverer' (pp. 74-5). A charming little tale about human foibles, which happily and affectionately it forgives. It reminds me very much of Prévert's 'Song of the snails on their way to a burial', or some of Jo-Ann Léon's work, naïve-looking but none too innocent.

When I decided to make a list of what I identified as the subject or theme or style of each poem in *Défier le destin,* a relatively small number of headings emerged. 'Children' were there, so was 'mother' (Carême was always close to his), as were 'Prévert-like' and 'surrealist echoes'. More substantial was the group of poems under the heading 'justice and peace'. The largest groups were 'silence', 'death', 'God', and biggest of all 'troubled state'. However you reclassify these subjective categories, and take into account inevitable overlaps, it seemed to me then – and seems more so on further re-reading – that for all Carême's religious faith, his delight in domesticity and the life circumscribed by safe boundaries (he only ever had one modest teaching job in Brussels, he stayed married to one woman, he was attached to his mother), he has a decidedly troubled side. I wonder just how convincingly religious faith came to his rescue as late in his life he wrote these poems which sought to defy destiny; just how much this gentle man, who never was required to fight a war, was gripped by feelings and premonitions of waste, desolation and even violence. The poems here do seem to reveal a shift from the orderliness and comfort of a known and trusted world towards looming silence and emptiness. Couldn't Carême find his one God any longer? I read somewhere that there is a strain of nascent pantheism in him, a view which doesn't surprise too much as one closes this volume. But whatever its power to disturb, his soul-searching is not conducted violently nor gratingly, but always with a technical and expressive grace which steers the reader (and perhaps the poet himself?) away from overbearing bleakness. It's not easy to find in Carême the signs of melancholy and self-pity, or minor key effects. Any sense that solitude is beckoning with its promise of suffering, and that God will not rise to the occasion, never manages to eclipse the delight that is provoked by a well-turned line. I think I'd like to call him a poet of tact. What he says may be disturbing, but the way in which he says it remains well-mannered.

Christopher Pilling impressed some years ago with *These Jaundiced Loves*, his dazzling translation of Tristan Corbière's *Les amours jaunes*. Altogether different poetry from Carême's, of course. Yet in the present volume he shows how sensitive is his ear to the nuances of a different kind of French, which he conveys in a different kind of English. While Pilling may be drawn in, as probably we all are, by the seductions of verse that rhymes, he has not routinely sought to match each rhyme one by one. Similarly, in the matter of metre, he has moved a respectable distance away from the French predilection for syllabics. He has rethought these poems in English, essential to do, paradoxically, if you're to be a faithful translator of the original *poem*.

With this intriguing Belgian poet and his accomplished English translator, Arc Publications have added another fascinating and valuable Visible Poet to its innovative series.

Martin Sorrell

DEFYING FATE
DÉFIER LE DESTIN

Le cœur pur

Il se contentait d'être
Heureux sans le paraître.
Et, se moquant des grands,
Il vivait comme un gueux,
Fuyait les gens sérieux
Et la gloire et l'argent.
On l'aurait volontiers
Arrêté, enfermé.

Mais quel homme au cœur pur
Ne traverse les murs?

Il avait du ciel
   à Alexis Dumoulin

Il avait du ciel dans la tête,
De la lune aussi dans le cœur.
Il était de toutes les fêtes
Avec ses lampions de couleur.
Dans l'ombre verte des feuillages,
Ses mains se changeaient en oiseaux.
Il se perdait dans son image
Comme une barque sur les eaux.
Mais il n'arrivait pas à dire
Pourquoi tant de choses si simples
Pour lui, si nues en leur candeur,
Lui procuraient tant de bonheur.

The pure in heart

Content to be happy
Without appearing so
And scorning the snappy
Dresser he lived like a hobo
Avoiding all the dead
Serious, the dead famous and the loaded.
One said: Let's get him
And lock him away. So did
Many others on a whim.

But what man whose pure heart never palls
Finds it hard to pass through walls?

He had sky
for Alexis Dumoulin

He had sky in his head,
And moon in his heart.
Whenever anyone fêted
Anything he'd be there from the start
With his Chinese lanterns.
In green leafy shade
His hands changed to gulls.
He got lost in his image
Like a boat the lake lulls
On its crystal clear waters.
But why, he couldn't say,
Did so many simple things,
So naked in their candour,
Seem to come on wings
And really make his day?

L'homme

L'homme et l'oiseau se regardèrent.
– Pourquoi chantes-tu? lui dit l'homme.
– Si je le savais, dit l'oiseau,
Je ne chanterais plus peut-être.

L'homme et le chevreuil se croisèrent.
– Pourquoi joues-tu? demanda l'homme.
– Si je le savais, dit la bête,
Est-ce que je jouerais encore?

L'homme et l'enfant se rencontrèrent.
– Pourquoi ris-tu ainsi? dit l'homme.
– Si je le savais, dit l'enfant,
Est-ce que je rirais autant?

Et l'homme s'en alla, pensif.
Il passa près du cimetière.
– Pourquoi penses-tu? dit un if
Qui poussait dru dans la lumière.

Et, pas plus que l'oiseau dans l'ombre,
Que le chevreuil dans la clairière
Ou que l'enfant riant dans l'air,
L'homme ne put rien lui répondre.

Il voulut dire…

Il voulut dire le jour
Avec des mots tels des tours
Vues de très loin sur les labours.

Il voulut dire la nuit
Avec des mots bien à lui,
Des mots aussi ronds que des nids.

The man

The man and the bird looked at each other.
– Why do you sing? said the man.
– If I knew that, said the bird,
I mightn't sing any more.

The man and the roe deer crossed paths.
– Why are you playing? asked the man.
– If I knew that, said the deer,
Would I go on playing?

The man and the child came face to face.
– Why are you laughing like that? asked the man.
– If I knew, said the child,
Would I laugh as much?

And the man went on his way, lost in thought.
He walked past the cemetery.
– Why are you thinking? asked a yew-tree
Growing bushy in the light.

And, no better than the bird in the shade,
The roe deer in the clearing
Or the child laughing,
Could the man give an answer.

He wanted to say…

He wanted to say day
With words like towers
Seen from a distance over ploughed fields.

He wanted to say night
With words that were his very own,
Words as round as nests.

Et dire aussi la bonté
Avec des mots généreux
Tel du soleil dans les yeux.

Alors, il trouva des mots
Si simples, si familiers
Que, pour partager le pain,

Il n'eut qu'à tendre les mains.

La liberté

Je suis la liberté,
Répétait-il, la liberté
Avec tous les dangers
Que je vais vous valoir
Et, pour me faire taire,
Il faudra me tuer.

Mais on le laissait faire,
On le laissait parler.
Il était bien trop solitaire
Pour amener l'homme à briser
Le cercle de fer et d'acier
Où l'injustice et la misère
L'avaient peu à peu enfermé.

Je suis la liberté,
Répétait-il encor.
Regardez-vous. Vous êtes morts.
Mais, comme on avait à manger,
On le laissait crier.

And to say goodness too
With generous words
Like sun in your eyes.

Well, he found words,
Such simple and familiar ones
That, to share bread,

He had only to reach out his hands.

Freedom

I am freedom,
He kept saying, freedom
With all the dangers
I'll point out to you
And, to shut me up,
You'll have to kill me.

But we let him carry on,
We let him speak.
He was too much a loner
To get man to break
The fetters of iron and steel
Into which injustice and need
Had gradually locked him.

I am freedom,
He kept repeating.
Just look at yourselves. You are dead.
But, as we had enough to eat,
We let him carry on shouting.

Le cri de la grive

De son immense clé, la nuit
Ouvrait comme un monde ébloui.

Lents et superbes, des nuages
Avançaient comme des rois mages

Au milieu d'un silence tel
Qu'on entendait frémir le ciel.

Sur les prés, le soleil mourait
Dans un tourbillon de reflets.

Seul, le cri furtif d'une grive
Perdue du côté de la rive

Lui rappelait encor parfois
Qu'il était à l'orée du bois.

Les illusions

J'ai mis mes illusions
En cage et voilà qu'elles chantent,
Dit-il, dans ma maison
Ainsi que des pinsons.

J'aurais peut-être bien mieux fait
D'aller les lâcher dans les champs,
Mais aurais-je jamais
Eté heureux comme à présent?

Pourtant, les jours de doute,
Sans hésiter, je les écoute
Pour trouver la sérénité

The cry of the thrush

With her enormous key, night
Opened a world we'll call all-bright.

Slow and superb, clouds were then
Advancing like three wise men

Through a silence deep enough to make
You hear the whole sky quake.

Over the meadows the sun was dying
In a whirligig of flying

Hues. A thrush, lost by the river bank,
Gave a ghostly call and he could thank

It for the fresh reminder that he could
Still be at the edge of the wood.

The illusions

I've shut my illusions in a cage
And they are singing, listen,
    He said, here in my house
    Like chaffinches.

Perhaps I'd have done better
To let them fly off over the brow
Of the hill, but would I ever
Have been as happy as I am now?

    And yet, on days of doubt,
I don't hesitate, I seek them out
    – For peace of mind.

Sans deviner que leurs chansons
Font naître d'autres illusions
    Encore plus rusées.

Il parlait pour tuer le temps

Il parlait pour tuer le temps,
Parlait pour se faire un écran
Entre lui-même et le néant,
Parlait sans comprendre pourquoi,
Les mains croisées et le front las,
La vie le tannait à tous vents,
Parlait comme doit parler Dieu
Qui ne sait plus bien ce qu'Il veut
Tant il y a de malheureux
A le supplier sous les cieux.

La même allée

Peu importe, lui disait-il,
L'endroit où je me trouverai.
Ne sommes-nous pas en exil
Parmi ces toits et ces vergers?

Que la fenêtre soit ouverte,
Que la fenêtre soit fermée,
C'est toujours la même allée verte
Que je suivrai à pas comptés.

I don't realise their every song
      Gives birth to a throng
Of other illusions more cunningly inclined.

He talked to kill time

He talked to kill time,
Talked to erect a screen
Between himself and the void,
Talked without grasping why,
Arms folded, furrowed brow,
Life drove him up the wall,
Cuffing him at every turn,
Talked as God must talk
No longer knowing what He wants,
No longer knowing how
So many unhappy folk
Could be begging for salvation now.

The same way

Makes no odds, he'd smile,
Wherever I happen to be
Aren't we all in exile
Under any roof or fruit tree?

Whether the window is open,
Whether the window is closed,
It's always the same green way,
      The path I chose.

Même si, comme l'hirondelle,
Je pouvais un jour m'envoler,
A quoi me serviraient des ailes
Qui ne sauraient pas où aller?

La bannière

Il aurait voulu imprimer
Sur la bannière de sa vie
Tout ce dont il avait envie
D'enseigner à ses héritiers.

Il la déploya en plein vent
Afin que ce qu'il écrirait
Soit plus naturel et plus vrai
Que scellé par un testament.

Mais un jour, il pleuvait à verse,
Un autre jour, il faisait froid.
Et la bannière resta là

Trouée comme un tonneau en perce.
Ce que firent ses héritiers
De ses biens pourtant séculiers.

Even if, like the swallow, I'm free
      To take off by and by
What good would wings be to me
If they don't know where to fly?

The banner

He'd have liked to spell them out
On his life's banner and flying,
All the things he was dying
To teach his descendants about.

He'd unfold it when big winds blew
So the words he wanted to write
Would look more natural, more true
Than in a will, sealed tight.

But one day it poured with rain,
Another, it was far too cold.
The banner lay there with a hole

In – like a barrel that's tapped.
Which is what his heirs did with his gains,
Ran through them in fact.

L'incrédule

— L'homme, c'est quelque chose,
　　Disait-il. Dieu n'est rien.
Cet oratoire en marbre rose
　　Le montre bien.

— Mais il n'est rien sans cause,
Lui rétorquait-on, amusé.
Un jardin ne sent pas la rose
　　Sans avoir de rosier.

— Cependant, je ne sens
Pas Dieu, même dans une église,
Répondait-il, mais bien l'encens
　　Que l'on idéalise.

　　On avait beau lui dire :
　　Dieu échappe à nos prises.
　　　　Il répondait :
Il est chaque jour dans la brise

Tant de choses qui nous échappent
Que l'on peut toujours les couvrir
Comme l'on couvre d'une chape
　　Les saints et les martyrs.

On s'habitue à tout

On s'habitue à tout, disait-il,
Avaler des oiseaux de plomb,
Cimenter les rives d'une île,
Voler, tête en bas, en avion.

The non-believer

Man's quite something, he opined,
        And God's nothing, over-rated.
Just look at that pink marble shrine
        Man has created.

Amused, someone retorted: – D'you suppose
        That anything is cause-free?
A garden can't smell of the rose
        If there's no rose-tree.

    Even in church I don't sense
    God's there – I don't feel
His presence, he said. I smell incense
        And man inventing an ideal.

It was no use telling him then
    That God is beyond our ken.
        For he would say:
          – Every day

In every breeze we could discover
        So many things we can't hope
To comprehend, which people can always cover
Up, like saints and martyrs with a cope.

You can get used to owt

You can get used to owt, he said,
Cementing the shores of an island,
Swallowing birds made of lead,
Flying, head down, over high land.

Mon père travailla trente ans
Derrière des grilles de banque;
Ma mère, encore plus longtemps
Dans une usine à Salamanque.

Mes frères firent la fortune
D'un grossiste en caisses de prunes.
Ma sœur a eu beaucoup à faire
Pour contenter son vieux notaire.

Et, quant à moi, n'en parlons pas!
Je suis encore militaire
Et, demain, je pars pour la guerre
Mitrailler sans savoir pourquoi.

La rue déserte

    La rue était déserte.
Les marronniers, avec leurs feuilles,
Faisaient de larges ombres vertes.

Elle a pensé: C'est bientôt l'heure
    Où Joseph va passer
Avec ses yeux rouges qui pleurent.

Mais Joseph était en retard.
Le temps de lui dire bonsoir,
Il était déjà reparti.

Alors, elle s'est demandé
    Ce qu'elle faisait là…

My father worked for thirty year
Behind a grill as a banker;
My mother – "I did more, my dear!" –
In a factory in Salamanca.

My brothers earned a fortune
Packing plums in packing cases.
My sister did her boss a boon
When he put her through her paces.

As for me, we'll say no more!
Still a soldier boy am I.
Tomorrow I go to fight a war,
To kill and not know why.

The empty street

      The street was deserted.
The horse chestnut trees
Made broad green shadows with their leaves.

She thought: It will soon be time
      For Joseph to be passing by,
His eyes red with crying.

But Joseph was late.
No sooner had she said good day
Than he was on his way.

So she asked herself what for,
      Why linger?

Ne sachant plus trop que vouloir
Elle a passé au doigt son dé,
   Et puis l'a retiré.

   Doucement, sur les feuilles
Sèches éparses sur son seuil,
Il a commencé à pleuvoir.

Dieu et le diable

Il posait des questions au diable,
Il posait des questions à Dieu.
Le diable étant le plus aimable,
Il cessa d'en poser à Dieu.

Mais qui peut se fier au diable!
Satan peignit l'enfer en bleu
Pour lui jouer un tour pendable
Et paria d'y installer Dieu.

Or Dieu qui joue cartes sur table
N'aime pas gagner à la diable.
S'il met parfois la main au feu,

C'est pour éviter que le diable,
Trompé à son tour par son jeu,
Ne prenne, pour atout, les cieux.

No longer knowing what to want
She put her thimble on her finger
    Then pulled it off again.

    Gently, on the dry leaves
Scattered by her front door
        It started to rain.

God and the Devil

He'd ask the Devil for info,
And God to give him the nod.
The Devil was never no-no,
So he gave up asking God.

But who can trust Old Nick!
When he painted hell sky-blue
He was playing a dirty trick,
He'd room for God there too!

Now, God plays cards-on-the-table,
Can never win by faking,
Will burn his fingers to be able

To prevent the Devil taking
Liberties, getting the hump,
Choosing heaven as trumps.

Ce rien de ciel
à Marcel Delmotte

Il y avait, sur la table, un gros pain;
A côté du pain, un couteau
Et, près du couteau, une pomme.
Et, devant le pain, le couteau, la pomme,
    Il y avait un homme.
Tout cela, dites-vous, n'a rien
Que de banal et même d'enfantin.
Mais cet homme était peintre.
Il peignit donc une table, un gros pain,
A côté du pain, un couteau
Et, près du couteau, une pomme.
Et il y mit ce rien de ciel
Qui fait que tout est essentiel.

La maison

Avec le vide des fenêtres,
Le vide à deux battants des portes,
Il construisit une maison
Qu'il plaça au-dessous d'un hêtre
Qui n'avait que des feuilles mortes.
Comme on le voyait au travers
De cette maison sans cloisons,
On crut qu'il vivait en plein air.
Il se faisait un arc-en-ciel
Comme ça pour la seule joie
D'y faire passer à la fois
Des autours et des hirondelles.

This dab of sky
for Marcel Delmotte

There on the table was a loaf;
By the loaf, a knife
And near the knife, an apple.
In front of loaf, knife and apple,
    Stood a man.
All of which, you say, is nothing
Special, is banal, childish even.
But this man was an artist.
So he painted a table, a loaf,
Next to the loaf a knife
And, near the knife, an apple.
Then he added this dab of sky
Making everything essential.

The house

With gaps for windows
And two gaps for double doors
He built a house
And put it on all fours
Beneath a beech tree
That only bore dead leaves.
As he could be seen wherever
He was in this no-wall house
People thought he lived
In the open air.
He made a rainbow for himself
Solely for the pleasure
Of having goshawks
And swallows fly through it.

Et il arrivait qu'un nuage
Vînt le saluer au passage.
Pourtant, quand la neige tombait,
Il aimait à se retrouver,
Seul à seul, avec son vieux cœur
Ronronnant tel un chat couché
Dans son étonnante demeure.

Les navires

Il arrive que des navires
Quittent peu à peu leur sillage
Et, sans qu'on puisse intervenir,
Gagnent lentement les nuages.

Quelquefois, un mousse pressent
Que c'est là son dernier voyage
Et sa main s'agrippe en tremblant
Au rebord froid du bastingage.

Tout se perd alors dans le ciel.
On attend longtemps des nouvelles
De ces navires que le sort

Choisit pour fendre l'univers,
Et leur étonnante lumière
Fait briller jusqu'au cœur des morts.

A cloud floated by
To greet him as it passed.
Yet, when snow fell,
He liked to be on his very own
With that good old heart of his
Purring like a curled-up cat
In his astonishing home.

Certain ships

Certain ships have been known to forsake
The sea, without our deciding what's allowed,
By rising little by little from their wake
And slowly attaining the clouds.

Sometimes, a cabin boy has a foreboding
That this will be his final trip
And his hand trembles when he's holding
The ship's cold rail tight as he can grip.

Then all gets lost at some great height
In the sky. For a long time people wait
For news of those ships that fate

Has chosen to split the world apart,
And their quite astonishing light
Causes even the dead to shine in their hearts.

Les chaînes

Je n'aime pas les chaînes,
Pas même celles que l'on met
Au cou des chiens,

Répétait-il.
Et, comme il se vantait
D'être avant tout un homme libre,

Le soleil traversant
La grille refermant
L'entrée de son jardin sauvage,

Lui noua tout à coup,
En sortant d'un nuage,
Sa chaîne d'ombre autour du cou.

Le peuplier

Enfant, il rêvait de monter
Sur le plus haut des peupliers
Afin de dominer le monde.

Et, chaque fois, ses mains dans l'ombre
Le trahissaient à mi-hauteur.

Mais toujours il recommençait,
Espérant, à force d'ardeur,
Arriver enfin au sommet.

Parfois, il passe dans l'allée
Où, enfant, il a tant joué.

Chains

I don't like chains,
Not even the ones they put
Round the necks of dogs,

He kept saying.
As he prided himself
On being above all a free man,

The sun, that shone through
The gate closing
The entrance to his wild garden

As it came out of a cloud,
Suddenly knotted
A chain of shadow round his neck.

The poplar

As a child he dreamt of climbing
To the top of the tallest poplar
So he could rule the world.

And, every time, his shadowy hands
Would let him down half way up.

But he would try again, and again,
Hoping, because of his passion,
To get to the top at last.

Sometimes he goes along the street
He played down so often as a kid.

Et, quand il voit le peuplier
Fuser au milieu de l'été,
Il a peine à se rappeler

Qu'alors, ivre de liberté,
Il s'acharnait à y monter.

La tête

Il disait ce qui lui passait
    Par la tête. Hélas!
Ce qui passait ne valait pas
Le poids de cette tête-là.

Elle se chargeait de carrosses,
    De reines, de fées.
Or qui ne sait que, pour les noces,
Dinde vaut mieux que sa fumée?

N'allez pas croire pour cela
Que c'était la tête d'un roi
Et qu'il se trouvait en Espagne

Où les châteaux ne coûtent rien.
Et d'ailleurs, même à la campagne,
Qui jamais reconnaît les siens?

And, when he sees the poplar
Burst into leaf in mid-summer
He finds it hard to remember

That, once, drunk on freedom,
He tried desperately to climb it.

In the head

He kept saying what passed
        Through his head. Alas!
What passed through it
Wasn't worth the time he gave to it.

It was chock-full of carriages,
        Of queens and fairy folk.
Now who doesn't know that, at marriages,
Turkey's worth more than its smoke?

Don't start believing it plain
That his was the head of a king
And he was building in Spain

Where castles don't cost a thing.
And, besides, even in Cockaigne,
Does anyone recognise his kin?

Que cherchait-il...

Que cherchait-il ainsi
Sans que jamais, au grand jamais,
   Il puisse définir
    Ce rien qui lui manquait?

   Espérait-il vraiment,
    Un jour, le rencontrer
Qu'il errait, si désemparé,
    Dans ce faubourg bruyant

   Où il marchait des heures
Avec, lui roulant dans le cœur,
    Ce seul grain acéré
Qu'il se devinait condamné,

Bon gré mal gré, à supporter?

La voix

Je ne parle pas pour moi,
Je prends simplement la voix
Qui dort dans votre inconscient,
Répétait-il tout le temps.

Mais sitôt qu'on l'écoutait,
On reconnaissait sa voix.
Ne devine-t-on un muguet
A son odeur dans le bois?

What was he looking for...

      What was he looking for like this,
Never able, when put on the spot,
         To be precise, to be specific
         About the whatsit he hadn't got?

      Did he really hope,
      One day, to come across it,
So down he could hardly cope,
So distraught, so at a loss it
         Was painful to see
Him wander in this noisy part of town

      Where he'd walk for hours on end
With this single sharp bit of grit that grated
         On his nerves, in such despair
That he saw himself condemned,

           Fated,
        Like it or not, to bear?

The voice

I'm not saying this for my sake,
It's the voice of your unconscious
And I'm rousing it – it wasn't awake.
So he kept telling us.

But when we heard how it went
We recognised it, we understood:
Like the lily of the valley's scent
Announces its presence in the wood.

C'était comme si le jour
Eblouissant de clarté
Naissait soudain sous ses pieds,

Comme s'il vous saisissait
Le bras pour aller plus loin
Que tout ce qu'on aimait bien.

Le monde est beau
à Fatima Lahbabi

Le monde est beau, répétait-il
      En souriant,
Même si la plupart le pillent
      Effrontément.

N'allez surtout jamais leur dire
      Que j'ai douté,
Ajoutait-il, car rien n'est pire
      En vérité.

Dites que je suis mort debout
Même si mon vieux cœur, à bout,
      Devait se plaindre.

Répétez-leur: Le monde est beau
Même si l'on tue les oiseaux
      Parmi les fleurs.

It was as if the day, waving a wand
Of dazzling brightness, was suddenly
Being born beneath our feet,

As if we were being taken by the arm
To be led on further, beyond
Everything we had loved so far.

The world is beautiful
for Fatima Lahbabi

The world is beautiful, protect it,
    Said his smile. You agree?
Even if most folk want to wreck it
    Quite shamelessly.

Never let them hear me curse
    The world, just their lack,
He'd add, for nothing could be worse
    Than that.

    Say that I died undeterred
Even if this old heart of mine
Were to murmur and turn sour.

Tell them yet again: the world is fine
And lovely, even if they kill the birds
    Among the flowers.

L'indigent

Il avait la faim pour assiette;
  La soif pour verre d'eau.
Il n'avait que des cris d'oiseaux,
  Dans le matin, pour miettes.
Et il vivait cahin-caha
Des sautes du vent, d'un parfum,
Des ultimes mots d'un défunt.
  Etonnés, les bourgeois,
Gorgés de crème et de foie gras,
  Se demandaient comment
Il pouvait vivre aussi longtemps
  De l'air du temps?

Le suicide

On le vit monter sur le toit
Et se laisser choir dans le vide.

Il est là, couché dans la rue,
Indifférent à la cohue
Des gens effarés qui affluent.

Et chacun de se demander
– Sa décision mûrement prise –
  Pourquoi il a laissé,
Dans sa minable chambre grise,
  Une lampe allumée.

The pauper

Hunger was his dinner-plate;
A glass of water his thirst.
In the morning his only crumbs
        The cries of birds.
He got along as best he could
With rough and ready gusts
Of wind, a scent, the last
Words of a dying man.
Amazed, the well-to-do, stuffed
Full of cream and pâté de foie gras,
        Wondered how
He could live so long
        On fresh air alone?

The suicide

People saw him climb on the roof
And throw himself off the top.

There he is, sprawled in the street,
Indifferent to the crush
Of frightened folk who've come rushing up.

And everyone is wondering why
– His decision being made
        Beforehand – why,
In his dingy grey miserable room,
        He's left the light on.

Les deux gamins

    Il sortit. Sur la ville,
Il recommençait à pleuvoir.
Tout le long du trottoir tranquille,
Il n'y avait personne à voir.

L'idée lui vint qu'il était seul
    Au cœur de la cité
Dans la grande allée aux tilleuls
Ordinairement si bondée.

    Il eut peur comme si
Vraiment il en était ainsi.
Et il se réjouit soudain
D'apercevoir deux grands gamins.

Il se précipitait vers eux
    Lorsqu'il les vit tous deux
Entrer dans un immeuble ancien.
Il ouvrit à son tour la porte.

Derrière, il n'y avait rien, rien
Que le ciel, rien que la rue morte.

Le misanthrope

Hélas! comme il n'aimait personne,
Personne, ici-bas, ne l'aimait.
Et tous ses secrets ne valaient
Guère mieux que feuilles d'automne
Qu'indifférent le vent emporte
Et disperse le long des portes.

The two strapping lads

        Out he went.
It was starting to rain again.
All along the quiet pavement
There was no one to be seen.

It occurred to him he was alone
At the heart of the city
In the wide tree-lined road
        Usually so busy.

He was afraid. Fearing
His loneliness would last,
It was suddenly cheering
To see two great big lads.

He dashed towards them.
When he saw both enter
An old tenement building
He followed them in.

Inside was nothing, nothing
But sky, and the dead street.

The misanthropist

Alas! as he didn't love a soul
No one on earth loved him.
And all his secrets were hardly worth
More than the autumn leaves
An indifferent wind is swirling
In doorways down the length of our road.

Sous le ciel noir

Ils n'avaient qu'à tendre, pour boire,
    Leurs mains ouvertes.
Ils se taillèrent un ciboire.

Ils n'avaient qu'à rire à la vie
    Pour s'émouvoir.
Ils se firent un ostensoir.

Ils n'avaient qu'à laisser la terre
    A son mystère.
Ils forgèrent un encensoir.

L'amour était leur meilleur gage.
    Mais pour y croire,
Il leur fallut, sous le ciel noir,
Créer un dieu à leur image.

Le mort et l'enfant

Brusquement, un enfant cria.
Etonné, le vent s'arrêta.

Tout environné de lumière,
Un mort sortait du cimetière.

Comme toujours, en pareil cas,
Personne ne le remarqua.

Un homme labourait son champ,
Un fermier triait son froment.

Une femme pendait son linge,
Son amie réparait des langes.

Under the threatening sky

They had only to cup their hands
        For a drink.
They shaped a ciborium.

They had only to laugh out loud at life
        To enjoy it.
They made a monstrance.

They had only to leave the earth
        To its mystery.
They moulded a censer.

    Love was their guarantee.
        But to believe in love,
They had, beneath the threatening sky,
To create a god in their own image.

The dead man and the child

All of a sudden, a child gave a shout.
Astonished, the wind blew itself out.

In a halo of light – the light that saves –
A corpse rose from one of the graves.

As usual, when such things chance,
No one gave him a passing glance.

One man went on ploughing his field,
A farmer went on sifting his yield.

A woman went on hanging out clothes,
Her friend was mending her pantihose.

Le vent se reprit à souffler
Réduisant le mort en poussière.

A la porte du cimetière,
L'enfant se remit à jouer.

La marche d'escalier

Oh! vous pouvez monter
Sans risque d'être dérangé

Afin de voir la ville
Se coucher comme un chien docile.

Je ne suis, disait-il,
Qu'une marche de l'escalier,

Et vous pouvez poser
Votre pied sur mon cœur tranquille.

D'ailleurs, ne suis-je né
Pour être sans cesse écrasé?

J'ai peur qu'au paradis,
Malgré ce qui me fut promis,

Toujours, je continue
A n'être, au milieu des nuées,

Pour les autres élus,
Qu'une marche de l'escalier

Montant vers la clarté.

The wind blew up again with a gust
Reducing the dead body to dust.

At the cemetery gates, just as before,
The child started to play once more.

One in a flight

   Oh! you can climb up on me
With no bother at all to see

   The town settle down
And curl up like a well-bred hound.

   For all I am, he would say,
Is one tread of a stairway,

   And you can put your foot
In however heavy a boot

   On my silent heart
For wasn't I here from the start

   To be constantly crushed?
I'm afraid that in heaven, despite

   All the promises made me
In earnest, I shall continue to be,

   In the clouds, for the other elect,
Just one step in a flight

   Climbing up to the light.

La charrette arrêtée

De très loin, il vit arriver
Une charrette et un cheval.
Le soleil brillait sur le val.

Quand la charrette s'arrêta,
Il s'aperçut avec effroi
Que personne ne la menait.

Le cheval paraissait normal.
Pourtant, lorsqu'il s'en approcha,
Soudain, la bête détala.

Et la charrette resta là,
Les bras levés vers la lumière,
Ainsi qu'une femme en prière
Implorant en vain le ciel bas.

Devant l'hôtel

Ils attendaient devant l'hôtel
Assis sur des chaises de paille.
Ils attendaient tel du bétail
Massé devant une écurie.
Une odeur de poulet rôti
Embaumait le massif de buis.
Au loin, la cloche d'une église
Sonnait longuement dans la brise.
Quelqu'un passait sans s'étonner
De voir tous ces gens demeurer
De longues heures sans bouger.
On entendait parfois grincer
Comme une bassine cuivrée,

The cart's held up

From afar off he saw
A cart and carthorse arrive.
The sun shone on the valley.

When the cart came to a stop,
He noticed with horror
That no one was driving.

The horse appeared normal.
Yet, when he approached,
Suddenly it clip-clopped off.

The cart stayed where it was,
Arms raised to the light,
Like a woman at prayer
Imploring the low sky in vain.

Outside the hotel

They were waiting outside the hotel
Seated on wicker chairs.
They were waiting like cattle do
Crowded outside a cowshed.
Through a clump of boxwood
Came wafts of roast chicken.
In the distance a church bell
Rang a long time in the breeze.
A passer-by showed no surprise
To see all these people sitting
Long hours not moving a muscle.
Sometimes there was a sound
Like a copper pan squeaking,

Et un reflet furtif passait
Entre les fentes d'un volet.
Personne, pourtant, ne bougeait.
Ils regardaient, ils attendaient.

Il riait

Il le savait: c'était
En vain qu'il s'adressait

Aux hommes qu'il aimait,
En vain qu'il priait Dieu.

Incroyablement bleu,
Le ciel restait muet.

Cependant, il riait
De se voir dans les yeux

De ceux qui le raillaient,
De ceux qui l'exploitaient

Sans savoir qu'ils étaient,
Eux, les plus malheureux.

And a stealthy gleam sneaked
Through the slits of a shutter.
Yet nobody moved.
They kept watching, they kept waiting.

He laughed

He knew: it was in vain
That he'd tried to explain

To the folk he loved, in vain
That he'd prayed to God, but he prayed.

Incredibly blue, the heavens
Stayed silent. However,

He laughed to see how he looked
In the eyes of those who mocked

And jeered him, those who derided
Him, exploited him or sided

Against him. Without it dawning on them
That they were the unhappiest of men.

Que cherchait-il?

Que cherchait-il, halluciné,
En tendant ainsi ses mains mortes
    Vers d'invisibles portes?

Il entendait derrière lui,
Mal étouffés par les hauts murs,
    Sourdre les derniers bruits
D'un faubourg treize fois impur.

    Pourtant, il avançait
Seul à la rencontre de l'ange
Qui, à l'orée de la forêt,
L'attendait depuis son enfance,
Les mains débordant de bleuets.

La mort de Marie

"Adieu" a dit Marie.
Elle a fermé les yeux
Pour ne plus voir les cieux
Luire sur la prairie.

C'est ainsi qu'elle est morte
Sans un mot, sans un cri,
Ses yeux comme une porte
Fermée sur ses soucis.

"C'est fait," a dit sa fille,
"Ça devait arriver.
Donnez-moi sa mantille,

What was he seeking?

What was he seeking, dazed,
There with his dead hands raised
    Towards invisible doors?

Behind him he could hear shouts
Hardly muffled by the high enclosure
    – The last sounds breaking out
From a suburb thirteen times impure.

    And yet he kept moving forward
Alone to meet the angel who stood
At the edge of the wood,
Having waited there since childhood,
Arms overflowing with cornflowers.

The death of Marie

"Goodbye" said Marie.
And she closed her eyes
So as not to see the sky
Lighting up the fields.

And that's how she died
Without a word, without a cry,
Her eyes shut like a door
Closed so she'd worry no more.

"It's over," said her daughter.
"It had to happen, though.
So hand me her cloak,

Je m'en vais la laver
Pour qu'elle se présente
A Dieu nette et décente
Comme sur ses portraits."

Et elle est demeurée
Seule sur les draps frais
Avec ses mains croisées
Sur son noir chapelet.

Son meilleur ami

Une pauvre chambre, une table,
Un verre d'eau, un lit minable,
Mais, enfin, cela lui suffit.
Ce qui lui manque, il se le dit
Comme si son meilleur ami,
Dieu lui-même, l'avait promis.
Vraiment, c'est comme s'il l'avait.
Il n'eut jamais d'autre secret
Et il rit lorsque nous doutons
De la clarté de sa raison.

I'll give it a wash
So she can say her hello
To God looking nice and posh
As she does in her photos."

And she lay there lost
And alone on the clean sheets
With her hands crossed
Over her black rosary.

His best friend

A poor room, a table,
A glass of water, a decrepit bed,
But they're all he needs.
Anything he lacks, he tells himself
What it is as if his best friend,
Say God himself, had promised it him.
So then, it's as if he actually had it.
He never had any other secret
And laughs away our doubts
About the clear-sightedness
Of his thinking.

Le collectionneur

Il bourrait ses tiroirs de livres;
Ses vases, de pesants bouquets.
Ses portes rutilaient de cuivres,
Ses murs n'étaient plus que portraits.
Si parfois on l'interrogeait
Sur cette manie qu'il avait
De s'entourer de tant d'objets,
Il riait de toutes ses dents
Et vous montrait votre cravate,
Puis ses pieds tout nus sur la natte
Qui recouvrait le pavement.

Il se sentit devenir...

Il se sentit devenir arbre.
    Ses jambes, tel du marbre,
        Tremblaient de froid.
    Ses mains étaient de bois.

    De jeunes feuilles vertes
        Perçaient sa peau.
    Quelques fleurs mal ouvertes
Rêvaient d'abeilles pour ses os.

    Saisi d'effroi
Devant cette paix infinie
    Qui l'avait envahi,

Il se raidit tant il craignit
    De perdre de surcroît
        Jusqu'au regret

De n'être plus ce qu'il était.

The collector

He stuffed his drawers with books;
His vases with heavy bouquets.
His doors glinted with brass plates,
His walls were nothing but portraits.
If from time to time we took
Him to task about this obsession
For not doing things by half,
This mania for the possession
Of objects galore, he would laugh
Uproariously and point to your cravat,
Then to his bare feet on the mat
You had covering the parquet.

He felt himself becoming…

He felt himself becoming
A tree. His legs, marble-cold,
Were all a-tremble. Hold
Them and his hands felt wooden.

Young green leaves set about
Pricking his skin.
A few flowers, not yet out,
Dreamed of bees for the bones he was in.

Seized with fright when faced
With this infinite peace
That invaded and embraced

Him, he stiffened up, so
Much so that he feared to lose
Even his sorrow

At no longer being what he'd been.

Le chasseur

Au fond, dormait-il
Lorsqu'il entendit
Sonner l'hallali?
De grandes fougères
Doraient de lumière
Le pied de son lit.
Des biches couraient
Sur les rideaux frais.
Dans la vapeur d'ambre
Flottant dans la chambre,
Il vit un fusil
Se braquer sur lui;
Et le coup partit.
Il se vit alors
Mourant sur son lit.
Rangés devant lui,
Au clair des bougies,
Les quatre chevreuils
Qu'il venait encor
De tuer la veille
Le veillaient, raidis.
Implacable, un cor
Sonnait l'hallali.

Je ne sais pas si Dieu...

Je ne sais pas si Dieu existe,
S'étonnait-il, ingénument.
Je ne suis pourtant pas moins triste
De ne pouvoir prouver comment
Ni pourquoi je le crois absent.

Il est des jours où il me semble
Qu'un ange me tient par la main,

The huntsman

Now, was he asleep
When he heard
The hunt's-up sounding?
Great big ferns
Gilded the foot of his bed
With light.
Deer ran
On the fresh-washed curtains.
In the amber mist
Floating in the bedroom,
He saw a rifle
Aimed at him;
And the shot went off.
He saw himself then
Dying on his bed.
Standing before him,
Rigid, in candlelight,
The four roe deer
He'd only killed
The day before
Watched over him.
Implacable, a hunting horn
Sounded the mort.

I don't know whether God…

I don't know whether God exists,
He'd say simply – it was no affront –
And I was no less sad when I kissed
The idea of God goodbye. I can't
Prove or say why I think he's absent.

There are days when it so happens
That an angel is holding my hand,

Mais c'est toujours quand le chemin
Rit en passant le long des trembles
Par un jour qui sent bon le thym.

Dès que je souffre, il m'abandonne
Pour s'en aller porter ailleurs
La part de bonheur qu'il me donne
Lorsque, d'accord avec mon cœur,
Je traverse des temps meilleurs.

Pour le diable, c'est autre chose.
S'il avait vraiment existé,
Il y a longtemps que les roses,
Pour se changer en argent rose,
Auraient délaissé leurs rosiers.

Le soir tombait

Il regarda par la fenêtre.
    La pluie cousait la terre
    Au ciel. Le soir tombait.
Un clairon sonnait la retraite.

Ne sachant plus alors que faire,
    Il ferma le volet,
Eteignit d'instinct la lumière,

Puis, se coucha de tout son long
Et attendit que le plafond,
    Sous l'éclat de l'éclair,

Dessine, étrangement parfait,
    Le petit trou formant,
Comme lorsqu'il était enfant,
    Un cœur dans le volet.

But it's always when the road is in raptures
As it passes along a line of aspens
And there's thyme scenting the land.

As soon as I'm suffering, he abandons me
To go off and offer elsewhere
The portion of happiness that is my share
When I'm in tune with my heart and free
To enjoy better times in his care.

As for the devil, that's another story.
If he had really existed
Each rose would long ago have insisted
On abandoning its rose-tree
To change into pink silver money.

Night was falling

He looked out of the window.
      Rain was stitching the ground
         To the sky. Day was about to go.
Retreat – came the sound

Of a bugle. What should he do now?
      He closed the shutter tight,
Instinctively put out the light,

Then, stretching full length, lay down
And waited for the ceiling to show,
      Each time lightning flashed,

The outline of the little hole,
That was, as when he was a lad,
      A strange but a
Perfect heart in the shutter.

La reine morte

Quand il entra dans cette tour
    Où la reine était morte,
Il n'entendit pas les verrous
Grincer lorsque s'ouvrit la porte.
Et, dans l'espèce de faux-jour
Où il montait les escaliers,
Le silence était si entier
Qu'il fut d'autant plus étonné,
En tournant au premier palier
    Où la reine était morte,
D'entendre brusquement la porte
Se refermer avec fracas
Et les verrous grincer trois fois.

Le sculpteur

Il prit un vieux chiffon usé,
Une feuille de peuplier,
Un clou d'autrefois, dédoré,
Une plume de geai brisée,
Un fin copeau de charpentier,
Un épi cueilli dans les blés,
La carcasse d'un encrier
Et il en fit une statue
Qu'on s'empressa d'inaugurer.

Elle éclaire toute la rue
Comme un pommier en liberté.

The dead queen

When he entered the tower
    Where the queen had died
He didn't hear the bolts screech
As the gate opened wide,
And when he climbed the stair,
In half light at that hour,
The silence was so complete
That he was all the more surprised
As he reached the first landing
    Where the queen had died
To suddenly hear the gate clanging
To and the bolts screech three times.

The sculptor

He took an old threadbare rag,
A poplar leaf,
An old-fashioned nail with the gilt rubbed off,
A jay's feather that had snapped,
A carpenter's off-cut,
An ear of wheat picked in the fields,
An inkwell stand
And with them he made a statue
People were quick to unveil.

It lights up the whole street
Like a free-flowering apple tree.

Le portrait

Sait-on encor ce qu'il regarde
Depuis bientôt près de cent ans?
Il était soldat de la garde
Dans quelque vague régiment.

C'était un ami, mais de qui?
Nul ne peut le dire à présent.
Les loups ont quitté les taillis,
Et il n'est plus de mère-grand.

Il tient ses gants dans une main
Tout aussi fièrement qu'avant,
L'autre main chaste reposant
Comme un chat blanc sur un coussin.

Est-on sûr d'ailleurs qu'il regarde
De ce côté-ci du couloir?
Il monte peut-être la garde
De quelque invisible manoir.

On sent bien qu'il est intraitable
Et qu'il tirerait aussitôt
Son grand sabre à glands du fourreau,
Dût-il voir s'avancer le diable.

L'indécis

Il mit le doigt entre deux pierres.
Puis, sans raison, le retira,
Cueillit quelques brins de bruyère,
Puis, ennuyé, les rejeta,
Se rassit, puis se releva
Et, sans raison, se demanda
Pourquoi il ne s'asseyait pas

The portrait

Hanging there for nearly a century,
On watch, for what? We're ignorant.
He was a soldier on guard duty
In some vague sounding regiment.

He was a good friend, but whose?
Those who might have told are past it.
The wolves have left the thicket
And there's no grandma left to lose.

He's holding his gloves in one
Hand proudly – still deems that best,
The other chaste hand is at rest
Like a white cat on a cushion.

Can we be sure he's looking hard
Down this side of the corridor?
He may just be standing there as guard
Of some invisible manor.

One senses he won't compromise
And that he'd straightway draw
His great tasselled sabre from its sheath
Should he see the devil take the floor.

The haverer

He stuck his finger between two stones.
Then, for no reason, pulled it out,
Picked a few sprigs of heather,
Then, bored, tossed them away,
Sat down again, then stood up
And, for no reason, wondered
Why he wasn't sitting

Un peu plus bas dans la lumière.
Puis, enfin, il se demanda
Ce qu'il irait faire plus bas.
Et, comme il ne le savait pas,
Il mit le doigt entre deux pierres
Et tout un temps le laissa là
Espérant bien savoir que faire
Quand il le tirerait de là.

La voûte des cieux

Croyant assister à la fête
Que célébraient sans fin les dieux,
    Il passa la tête
A travers la voûte des cieux.

Quelle ne fut pas sa surprise
De voir le ciel aussi désert
    Qu'une salle grise
Abandonnée à la poussière.

    Un silence infernal
Régnait sur une plaine nue.
    Pas un oiseau en vue.

Les cieux, la lune, les étoiles
    Et jusqu'aux moindres nues,
    Tout avait disparu.

A little lower down in the light.
Then, at length, he wondered
What he would do down there.
And, as he had no idea,
He stuck his finger between two stones
And left it there for quite a while
Hoping he'd know what to do
When he pulled it out again.

The heavenly vault

Thinking he'd join in the fun and games
Of the gods which never came to a halt
    He put his head up
Into the heavenly vault.

Imagine his great surprise
To see that heaven was just
As empty as a drab grey room
    Abandoned to dust.

    An infernal silence
Reigned over a bare expanse.
    Not a bird to be seen.

The sky, the stars, the moon
And each little cloud between
    – Everything had gone.

Sur le quai

– Vois-tu le trou dans la falaise?
– Je ne vois briller que des pierres.
– Vois-tu le ciel virer au vert?
– Non, un nuage allant à l'aise.
– Vois-tu les mouettes tourner?
– Non, je vois les galets rouler.
– Vois-tu au loin ce haut voilier?
– Et toi, cet horizon voilé?

Ils parlaient ainsi sur le quai
Comme ils en avaient l'habitude
Avec beaucoup de dignité
Et même de sollicitude,
Mais sans jamais, au grand jamais,
Aimer ce que l'autre voyait.

Les cimetières

Il regardait les cimetières
Où, tels des oiseaux alignés,
De grandes croix étaient posées.
Mais qui, en ce vaste univers,
A jamais pu être comblé!
Et il riait sachant combien
– Croyant tout mener à leur guise –
Les vivants ne devinent rien
De ce qui échappe à leur prise.

On the quay

– You see that hole in the cliff?
– All I see is stones gleaming.
– You see the sky turning green?
– No, just a cloud drifting by.
– You see the seagulls wheeling?
– No, I see pebbles rolling back.
– You see that tall ship in the distance?
– And you, the horizon veiled in mist?

They talked like this on the quay
As was their wont
With a great deal of dignity
And even solicitude,
But without ever, no not ever,
Enjoying what the other could see.

Cemeteries

He looked in at cemetery gates
Where, aligned like birds on wires,
Large crosses stood in state.
But who, in this huge universe of ours,
Has ever triumphed over the fates!
And he laughed, knowing how much men
Think they can take everything in their stride.
The living are taken for a ride
When it comes to things beyond their ken.

A quoi bon s'en faire!

Des enfants criaient dans la cour.
Il tendit les bras aux enfants.

Des bruants montaient dans le jour.
Il tendit les bras aux bruants.

Le soleil dansait sur les toits.
Il tendit les bras au soleil.

Le ciel coulait dans la rivière.
Il tendit au ciel, les deux bras.

Mais ni le ciel, ni les enfants,
Ni les bruants, ni la rivière,

Ni le jour ne le regardèrent.
Cependant, à quoi bon s'en faire!

Ne tendait-il les bras à Dieu
Présent derrière chaque chose

Comme le parfum sous la rose?

La fermière

Ah! cette fois, ça y est bien,
Disait Juliette, la fermière.
C'est quand il faut rentrer les foins
Que la pluie choisit notre coin.

Elle passait ses grosses mains
Sur son long tablier de toile,
Puis allait voir si son cheval
Avait son râtelier bien plein.

What's the good of worrying!

Children were shouting in the yard.
He held out his arms to the children.

Buntings were flying up in daylight.
He held out his arms to the buntings.

The sun was dancing on the rooftops.
He held out his arms to the sun.

The sky was flowing into the river.
He held out his arms to the sky.

But neither the sky, nor the children,
Nor the buntings, nor the river,

Nor the daylight noticed him.
But, what's the good of worrying!

Wasn't he holding out his arms to God
Present behind all that exists

Like scent at the heart of a rose?

The farmer's wife

Ah! yet again, it's not our day,
Sighed Juliette, the farmer's wife, it is not!
Just when we've got to bring in the hay
The rain chooses our little spot.

Wiping her huge hands down her coarse
Cotton apron, a long one but that didn't stop her,
She rushed off to see whether her horse
Had its trough full enough of fodder.

Et, dès que les vaches rentraient
Toutes trempées dans le jour terne,
On ne voyait plus sous l'averse

Que le bas de son masque inquiet
Où des gouttes d'eau scintillaient
Dans la clarté de la lanterne.

Il avait...
    à Robert Merget

Il avait sur les bras des grives,
    Beaucoup de grives.
Il avait beau lever les bras,
Les grives ne s'envolaient pas.

Il avait dans le cœur des faons,
    Beaucoup de faons,
Et, bien que son cœur fût étroit,
Les faons non plus ne fuyaient pas.

Il avait dans l'âme du ciel,
    Beaucoup de ciel.
Et pourtant la mort était là
Qui l'attendait au coin du bois.

And, no sooner were the cattle in for the night,
Soaked to the skin on the dullest of days,
Than you could only glimpse in the storm

The lower part of her worried face
On which drops of water had formed
And were glinting in the bright lantern light.

What he had
    for Robert Merget

On his arms he had song thrushes,
    A lot of thrushes.
He raised his arms in vain,
The thrushes didn't fly away.

In his heart he had young deer,
    A lot of fallow deer.
And, though his heart and mind were narrow,
They stayed, did the fallow.

In his soul he had the heavens,
    A lot of heaven.
Yet death was there as well
Waiting to meet him on the fell.

On le laissait dire

Le temps, prétendait-il,
Je le tends comme un fil
Et le courbe à ma guise.

L'espace, affirmait-il,
Je le tasse en un coin
Et le réduit à rien.

Mais on le laissait dire.
A quoi pouvait servir
Des ouvrages si vains?

Ne mourrait-il en somme
– Toute eau court au moulin –
Comme font tous les hommes!

Le mot

Un mot, un seul, nous disait-il...
Et tous cherchaient à deviner
Ce mot qui devait leur ouvrir
Les portes d'or de l'avenir,
Ce mot que Dieu tenait secret
Dans on ne sait quel lourd coffret,
Ce mot-clé sur lequel jamais
Deux personnes ne s'accordaient.

They let him say it

Time, he claimed, see –
I tense it like a wire
And bend it as I fancy.

Space, he kept affirming,
I heap it in a corner
And squash it down to nothing.

But they let him say it.
What use could such
Vain actions be?

Wouldn't he end up dead
– All water races to the mill –
As every man will!

The word

One word, just one, he'd say to us...
And everyone would try to guess
This word that would open for them
The golden gates to the future,
This word that God kept secret
In some heavy-lidded casket,
This key-word about which
No two persons ever saw eye to eye.

Il se souvint

Il se souvint d'une haie de troènes,
De la porte d'un four à pain,
D'un long banc où il s'asseyait
Dans un jardin soûl de bleuets,
D'un nuage blanc qui glissait
Lentement au-dessus des pins...
Mais tout cela triste, inutile,
Dans le coin perdu d'une ville
Clouée au cœur de son passé
Comme un morceau d'éternité.

L'envie

D'où lui venait cette envie
   De construire une échelle
Qui monterait jusqu'au soleil?
Avait-il, dans une autre vie,
   Eté fleur de soleil?
Il se le demandait parfois
Tandis qu'il rabotait sans fin
   Dans cet atelier froid
Où tout lui paraissait mesquin.
Ô secrète cosmogonie,
Ne voyait-il pas dans ses vitres
Poudroyer un couchant si rouge
   Que le bord de sa gouge
Brusquement se prenait à vivre?

He remembered

He remembered a privet hedge,
The oven door of a bakery,
A long bench he used to sit on
In a garden heady with cornflowers,
A white cloud gliding
Slowly over the pines…
But all of these are sad, of no avail,
In the out-of-the-way corner of a town
Pinned to the heart of his past
Like a scrap of eternity.

The desire

Where did it come from then,
This desire of his to build a ladder
That would reach to the sun?
Had he been a sunflower
In another life? he sometimes wondered
While planing things down non-stop
In his cold carpenter's shop
Where everything seemed no-good.
O secret cosmogony!
Out of his windows didn't he see
A setting sun rise up in clouds
Of dust so red that the knife-
Sharp edge of his gouge
Suddenly came to life?

Il se dépêchait de rire

Il se dépêchait de rire
Pour un rien, comme un enfant.
Avec la vie, au tournant,
Ne faut-il s'attendre au pire?
Quant à la mort, il savait
Qu'il devait s'en méfier.
La mort eut-elle jamais
Les rieurs de son côté?
C'est pourquoi il riait tant.
Quand on a fini de rire,
On a bien raison de dire,
Hélas, que c'est pour longtemps.

Il se demanda pourquoi

Il se regarda dans la glace.
Sa barbe noire avait grandi.
Puis, il vit que son ongle aussi,
Celui du pouce, avait grandi.

Il examina les ciseaux,
Puis le rasoir et puis le pain
Luisant sur la nappe à carreaux.

Il vit une croix sur le pain,
Une croix taillée au couteau.

Et il se demanda soudain
Pourquoi c'était l'ongle du pouce
Qui grandissait ainsi en douce,

Pourquoi un peu de sang coulait
Sur sa joue quand il se rasait,
Pourquoi même il se regardait.

He was quick to laugh

He was quick to laugh at something
Trivial, like a child would.
When it comes to life though, at every turning,
You should expect the worst, you should.
As for death, he really knew
He ought to keep it at arm's length.
Did death ever have a crew
Of jokers to reinforce his strength?
Which is why he laughed so much.
When you've finished laughing, fine,
You've every reason to say such
As: My God, that's that for a long long time.

He wondered why

He looked at himself in the glass.
His black beard had grown.
Then he saw his nail had too,
His thumbnail, that is.

He examined the scissors,
Then the razor, then the bread
Tempting there on the check cloth.

On the bread he saw a cross
That had been cut with a knife.

And he suddenly wondered
Why it was his thumbnail
That grew surreptitiously,

Why a little blood ran
Down his cheek when he shaved,
Why he even looked at himself.

Au cadran de l'éternité
à Géo Libbrecht

Quelle heure pourrait-il bien être
Au cadran de l'éternité?
Demandait, mourant, un poète.
Et, se tournant vers la fenêtre

Où se levait le jour d'été,
Il reprit d'une voix inquiète:
Quelle heure pourrait-il bien être
Au cadran de l'éternité?

Mais seul, dans son vieux cœur en fièvre,
L'écho de sa voix inquiète
Qui ne pensait qu'à le calmer
Ne parvint qu'à lui répéter:
Oui, quelle heure à l'éternité?

Avec les yeux du cœur

Il resta devant sa fenêtre
Et, malgré les volets fermés,
Il essaya de reconnaître
Qui, dans la rue, avait passé.

Il épia les moindres bruits.
Ne se fiant qu'à ses oreilles,
Il parvint à deviner qui
Se promenait dans le soleil.

Enfin, devenu maître en l'art
De voir, ainsi qu'en un miroir,
Les gens avec les yeux du cœur,

On eternity's clockface
for Géo Libbrecht

What time could it possibly be
On the clockface of eternity?
A dying poet asked
And, turning towards the window

At the dawn of a summer's day,
Said once more in a worried way:
What time could it possibly be
On the clockface of eternity?

But, alone, with his old heart
In turmoil – he had no choice –
The echo of his worried voice
Wanting to calm him down again
Only managed the same refrain:
Yes, what time in eternity?

With the eyes of his heart

He stayed at his window
And, despite the shutters being shut,
He tried to get to know
Who was passing in the street.

He picked up the slightest sounds.
He would guess, by relying
On his ears alone, who was out
Walking in the sunshine.

Eventually, now master
Of the art of seeing, as in a mirror,
People with the eyes of his heart,

Il finit par ne plus voir ceux
Qui passaient, ivres de rancœur,
Que marchant sur le bord des cieux.

Celui qu'il attendait

Il ne savait pas s'il viendrait,
Encor moins s'il était venu.
Il attendait sans amertume,
Les pieds tournés vers les chenets.

Un matin, on heurta la porte.
Il ouvrit. Un homme avançait
Aussi léger qu'une âme morte.
Il vint s'asseoir près des chenets

Et demeura ainsi, muet,
Longtemps, se chauffant près du feu,
En le regardant dans les yeux.

Mais lorsque soudain l'inconnu
Sortit sans le moindre bruit,
Il se demanda si celui

Qu'il attendait était venu.

He ended up by never
Seeing the ones drunk on rancour
Walking anywhere but the edge of heaven.

The one he was waiting for

He didn't know whether he would come,
Even less whether he had come.
He waited without bitterness,
His feet turned towards the firedogs.

One morning, there was a knock at the door.
He opened. A man stepped in
As insubstantial as a dead soul.
He came and sat by the firedogs

    And stayed there, dumb,
For a long time, warming himself by the fire,
Looking him straight in the eyes.

But when the stranger suddenly
    Left quite soundlessly,
He wondered whether the one

He was waiting for had been and gone.

L'écrivain

Je sais mieux que vous, disait-il,
    Que la vie est tragique,
    Que tout ce que j'écris
N'est ni plus juste, plus utile
    Qu'un labeur de fourmi.
Je sais, ma joie est sans raison.
    Mais je ne puis rien faire
Si l'univers ne semble là,
Avec ces entrelacs de ronces,
Que pour m'inonder de lumière.

Rien dans les mains

Rien dans les mains, rien dans les poches,
Rien dans la cour, rien au grenier,
Rien au seuil béant de sa porte,
Rien non plus le long de la rue,
Vide des seuils gris jusqu'aux nues.
Alors, ces pas qui s'approchaient,
Cette odeur qui se répandait
Et cette voix qui appelait?
Et il se souvint de sa mère
Avec une telle acuité
Qu'il la revit dans la clarté
Penchée sur la grande soupière
L'étoilant de vapeur dorée.

The Writer

I know better than you do, he'd say,
That life is tragic,
That everything I write
Is neither more truthful nor more useful
Than the labours of an ant.
I know, my happiness has no reason.
But I can't do a thing about it
If the universe seems to be here
With these tangles of brambles
Just to flood me with light.

With nothing in his hands

With nothing in his hands, nothing in his pockets,
Nothing in the yard, nothing in the attic,
Nothing in his yawning doorway,
And nothing all the way along the street
But an emptiness of dismal doorways as far as eye could see,
What then of these approaching footsteps,
This odour drifting over
And this voice calling?
And he remembered his mother
So incredibly clearly
That he saw her again, brightly lit,
Bent over the large soup tureen
Which swathed her in golden steam.

Mélanie

C'est que mes jambes ne vont plus,
Disait Mélanie en riant.

Elle était comme la statue
De la joie plantée dans la rue.

Et elle faisait des miracles.
Le bonheur n'en est-il pas un?

C'est que mes jambes ne vont plus,
Disait Mélanie, mais j'ai eu

Tout ce que le ciel peut donner
A qui n'a que sa pauvreté.

Et elle riait de plus belle
En croquant une mirabelle.

Le squelette

Que peut-on quand paraît la mort?
Et il perçut au loin dans l'ombre
Une voix sourde comme un cor
Qui essayait de lui répondre:
"Rien! eût-on dans la main tout l'or
    Amassé dans le monde."

Et, tenace, il imagina
De peindre un grand squelette en blanc.
Alors, il se planta devant
Et l'interrogea calmement.

Melanie

My legs don't work any more,
Said Melanie with a laugh.

She stood like the statue
Of joy planted there in the street.

And she performed miracles.
Isn't happiness one of them?

My legs don't work any more,
Said Melanie, but I have had all

That the heavens can give
To one who's only poverty to live with.

And she laughed with such good humour
As she sat sucking a satsuma.

The skeleton

What when death appears?   What's to be done?
And from the distant shadows came
A voice like a muffled horn
In reply: "Nothing! It would be the same
    If one owned
        All the gold in the world."

And, grimly, he imagined
Painting a large skeleton white,
Then, parking himself right
    In front questioned
It as calmly as he might.

Le squelette le regarda.
Et il se vit dans les trous noirs
De ses yeux comme en un miroir.

Les cieux

    Les cieux s'étant cassés,
On en ramassa les morceaux
Et l'on crut que c'était assez
D'en réajuster les carreaux.

    On eut de bonnes pluies,
Du soleil tant qu'on en voulut,
Mais comme toujours des ennuis
Et du mal plus qu'il n'en fallut.

    Et, bien qu'il fût la cible
De tous les projets d'avenir,
Dieu là-haut restait impassible.
Il n'eut pas à s'en repentir.

    Il devint Allah, Thor,
Wotan, Jésus au mont Thabor.
Même les plus amers se firent
Un dieu bon à n'en plus finir.

The skeleton looked back
At him and he saw himself in the black
Holes of its eyes as in a looking glass.

The heavens

    The heavens having broken,
People picked up the pieces
And thought it enough – it was a token –
To put the panes back in their places.

    They had good enough rains,
Sun as much as they wanted,
But as always they were haunted
By worse things – life's real banes.

    And, although he was present
In all plans for the future – how to live –
The Lord above remained impassive.
He had no cause to repent.

    He became Allah, Thor,
Wotan, Jesus on Mount Tabor.
Even the bitterest folk understood
They could have a god who was nothing but good.

L'angoissé

Mes parents auraient-ils œuvré en vain
Et parcouru en vain tant de chemins,
Mes enfants travailleraient-ils en vain,
Et leurs enfants referont-ils en vain
Tous ces chemins qui ne mènent à rien,
    Moi-même ai-je vécu en vain?

    On aurait voulu le confondre.
Mais nul ne trouvait rien à lui répondre.

La troupe d'anges

Il crut que c'était à sa droite
Que chantaient une troupe d'anges.
Mais non – comme c'était étrange –
A sa gauche aussi ils chantaient.

Il crut que c'était dans sa chambre
Que chantaient une troupe d'anges.
Mais non – comme c'était étrange –
Ils chantaient aussi dans la grange.

Il crut que c'était à sa table
Que chantaient une troupe d'anges.
Mais non – comme c'était étrange –
Ils chantaient aussi dans l'étable.

Alors, il se mit à genoux
Et pria pour mieux les entendre.
Mais alors – que c'était étrange –
Tout se tut au fond de lui, tout.

Man in anguish

Have my parents worked in vain,
Explored so many avenues in vain,
Are my children working hard in vain,
And will their children gain
Nothing from going with the grain
In all the enterprises whose end is all too plain,
    Will I myself have lived in vain?

    We wanted to chase his ideas away
But no one could think of anything to say.

The band of angels

He thought he heard them on his right,
A band of angels, singing with might
And main, but no – a strange to-do –
They were singing on his left side too.

He thought he heard them in his room,
A band of angels – and, I presume,
Nowhere else. No, it's strange to tell –
They were singing in the barn as well.

He thought he heard them at his table,
A band of angels – not in the stable.
No, yet how strange, for I'm telling you –
They were singing in the stable too.

So, obeying offices to the letter,
He knelt and prayed to hear them better.
But – how strange, unsanctified,
Everything fell silent deep inside.

L'aube

L'aube enterrait au fond du ciel
Les dernières étoiles mortes.
Elle a ouvert sa lourde porte
Et regardé dans la ruelle.

Toujours le premier au labeur,
Le fils de Françoise est passé.
Elle s'est dit: "Il est sept heures,
Je m'en vais moudre le café."

Mais les petites nues au ciel
Etaient si roses, si joufflues;
Les cris aigus des hirondelles,
Si vifs au-dessus de la rue,

Qu'elle est encore demeurée
Comme ça, longtemps, sans penser
A rien, ses vieilles mains
Sur son tablier de satin.

Et tout à coup, elle a toussé,
S'est aperçue qu'elle avait froid.
Alors, elle est vite rentrée,
A refermé sa porte à clé,

Puis a préparé, en tremblant
De hâte, le café qu'on boit
A petits coups dans le bol blanc
Quand il brûle encore les doigts.

Dawn

Dawn was burying the last dead
Stars in the depths of the sky.
She opened her door, heavy as lead,
And looked down the lane. By and by,

Always first to get to work,
Françoise's son was on his round.
She said to herself: "It's seven o'clock,
Time I got the coffee ground."

But the little clouds in the sky
Were so pink and chubby-cheeked;
The swallows' cries so high-
pitched as they swooped down the street

That she stood transfixed
For quite a while, not a thought in
Her head, her old hands cricked
Against her satin apron.

Then suddenly she coughed,
Realised how cold she was,
Went back in at speed,
Turned the key in the lock.

Hands trembling in her haste,
She then prepared the coffee
– To be drunk in little sips
So's not to burn fingers and lips.

Baptiste

"Je vais mourir", a dit Baptiste,
"Vous pouvez repartir tranquille.

Oh! ne dérangez pas mon fils!
A quoi cela servirait-il?"

Il a longuement regardé
Un portrait sur la cheminée,

Son portrait où, jeune soldat,
Il regardait droit devant soi

Avec des yeux prêts à dompter
La vie qu'il allait affronter.

Et c'est avec les mêmes yeux,
Ouverts tout grands sur la clarté,

Qu'il a regardé sans ciller
La mort entrer et approcher.

Le tiroir

Il rouvrit le tiroir fermé de sa jeunesse.
Une avenue monta ainsi qu'une promesse
Dans un tohu-bohu de vals et de coteaux.
Un enfant y courait avec un grand cerceau.
Au loin, dans l'ombre verte, un cercle de lumière
Brillait mieux qu'une lampe au creux d'un lampadaire.
Et ni soleil ni pluie, rien que le ciel tranquille
Qui s'étendait partout comme l'envers d'une île.
L'enfant courait toujours. Les arbres reculaient.

Baptiste

"I'll soon be dead," said Baptiste,
"Go, let that put your mind at ease.

Oh! don't bother my son, no need to!
What good would that possibly do?"

He looked for ages at himself
In a photo on the mantelshelf,

Then he was a young recruit
Looking straight ahead, en route,

With eyes alert, to put in its place
The life he was about to face.

And it's with the very same eyes,
Wide open to what might arise,

That he watched without fear
Death come in and draw near.

The drawer

He opened the closed drawer of his youth.
A child was running along with a hoop
Up an avenue which rose like his hopes
In a rum jumble of valleys and slopes.
In the distance, in green shadow, a circle of light
Shone, like the bulb in a street lamp, but so bright
That neither sun nor rain could dim it, only the quiet sky
That spread everywhere, even the antipodes.
The child was still racing past receding trees,

Et il n'entendait rien que le frais gazouillis
D'un oiseau deviné, caché dans les taillis,
Oiseau qui le suivait tout comme s'il était
Son cœur battant au chaud dans l'odeur des genêts.

Le mur blanc

Il avait beau voir les eaux luire
Chaque matin dans le soleil
Plus hallucinant que la veille,

Suivre du regard une fille
Qui passait si légère qu'elle
Avait tout l'air d'une hirondelle,

Il savait très bien que la vie
Etait ce mur blanc de soleil
Garni de tessons de bouteilles,

Ce mur blanc derrière lequel,
Quoi qu'il pût faire, il ne pourrait
Jamais voir ce qui se passait.

Vous moquez-vous?

Vous moquez-vous? lui dit la mer.
Pas du tout, lui dit le bateau.

Vous moquez-vous? dit le bateau.
Pas du tout, lui dit la lumière.

And all he could hear were the fresh rushes
Of birdsong and the bird hidden in the bushes
Following him, as if his heart were out there
Beating in the warm broom-scented air.

The white wall

Although he saw the water shimmer
Every morning in the sun – more
Staggeringly beautiful than the day before,

Although he pursued a girl with his eyes
As she passed so light of foot that to follow
Her was as hard as pursuing a swallow,

He knew perfectly well that life
Was this sun-whitened wall rife
With stuck shards of broken bottles,

So whatever he did, he never
Could see what was happening
Behind it, saw nothing whatsoever.

You pulling my leg?

You pulling my leg? asked the sea.
No way, said the boat.

You pulling my leg? asked the boat.
No way, said the limber.

Vous moquez-vous? dit la lumière.
Pas du tout, lui dit le marin.

Vous moquez-vous? dit le marin.
Pas du tout, dirent les galets.

De qui se moque-t-on là-bas?
Cria soudain le vent furieux.

Il frappa du poing sur la plage:
Tout se tut, de la terre aux cieux.

On disait

Comme il n'en faisait qu'à sa tête,
On disait qu'il était poète.
Indifférent, il s'en moquait.
Il n'écoutait, il ne voyait
Que ce que son cœur indécis
Voyait ou entendait pour lui.
A ceux qui riaient de le voir
Interroger le vent du soir,
Il répondait sans s'émouvoir:
"Ne suis-je pas ce que vous êtes
De l'autre côté du miroir?"

You pulling my leg? asked the limber.
No way, said the sailor.

You pulling my leg? asked the sailor.
No way, said the shingle.

Whose leg are they pulling down there?
Yelled the furious wind, going spare,

Thumping the beach with his upper hand:
All fell silent, in the sky, on sea and land.

What they said

He followed his every whim,
So poet is what they called him.
He was indifferent, offhand,
Not listening – he could only stand
To see what his indecisive mind
Saw or heard for itself.
To those who laughed to see him
Questioning the evening wind,
He answered without a flicker
Of emotion: "Am I not your replica
On the other side of the mirror?"

Faut-il s'étonner?

Qu'il se grattât l'oreille
Avec un tournevis
Ne prouve rien qui vaille.
D'autres, en plein soleil,
Le font avec un lis.

Qu'il trouvât que la nuit
A une queue qui traîne
Jusque dans les fontaines
Ne peut rien contre lui.
D'autres croient en la veine.

Mais qu'il osât crier
A la face du monde
Que l'on a étranglé
La justice dans l'ombre,
Qui – faut-il s'étonner? –

Pourrait lui pardonner.

Il ne parlait que du ciel

Il ne parlait que du ciel,
Des prés, des champs, des forêts,
Du soleil, des hirondelles.
Et il trouvait notre monde
Si beau qu'il le proclamait,
Sans se lasser, à la ronde.

"Peut-être y a-t-il un Dieu",
Répétait-il, mi-sérieux,
Mi-moqueur, "mais, entre nous,
Ne doit-il pas trouver drôle

Should we be surprised?

The fact that he'd scratched his ear
With a screwdriver
Would prove nothing that matters.
Other folk, in full view,
Do it with a lily.

The fact that he'd found night
Has a tail that drags
Up to and into fountains
Would be nothing against him.
Others believe in luck.

But that he'd dared to shout
Out for everyone to hear
That justice has been strangled
In some dark corner,
Who – and should we be surprised? –

Could possibly forgive him?

All he talked of…

All he talked of was the sky,
The meadows, the fields, the forests,
The swallows and the sun,
And he considered our world
So beautiful that he proclaimed it,
Without ever tiring, to everyone.

"Perhaps there is a God,
He kept saying, half serious,
Half mock, but, *entre nous*,
Mustn't he find it rather odd

Que l'on se mette à genoux
Pour le voir tenir son rôle,
D'ailleurs le même partout?"

Il mit son cœur

Un jour, il mit son cœur
Cuire comme un homard,
Puis le mangea le soir
Sans herbes et sans beurre.

Mais une fois sans cœur,
Il n'eut plus faim de rien
Pas même du lapin
Qu'il arrosait de vin.

Et il se mit à boire,
Mais que peut la boisson?
C'est le cœur qui doit croire
Qu'être soûl a du bon.

Que peut-il désormais
Désirer que la mort?
Mais que vaut une mort
Subie sans un regret?

That people keep kneeling
To see him acting his part,
As it's the same one everywhere?"

He put his heart

One day, he put his heart
In to cook like a lobster,
Then ate it at night
Without herbs or butter.

But once he was heartless
Hunger went into decline,
He even lost it for the rabbit
That he'd wash down with wine.

So he took to the drink,
Only what can booze do?
The heart's got to think
Being drunk's good for you.

From now on all he's fit
For is a desire for death?
But is a death worth it
If suffered with no regret?

Il se revoyait

Il se revoyait chaque fois
Assis au pied d'une aubépine
A travers laquelle les toits
Scintillaient, couronnés d'épines.

Une route s'en allait seule
Traversant de hautes moissons
Pour se perdre près d'un tilleul
Derrière l'immense horizon.

Un homme qu'il croyait connaître,
Tant il était pareil à lui,
Avançait, lassé, sous les hêtres
Dont l'ombre couvrait les pâquis.

Et il se demanda, inquiet,
S'il n'était pas cet homme-là
Qui s'en allait sans fin là-bas
Vers la nuit qui ne venait pas.

Le canot

Ne va pas si loin, crie la mère.
Pourtant, déjà dans son canot,
L'enfant gagne la haute mer
Et n'écoute plus un seul mot.

La vague rit de son audace,
Le vent l'aide autant qu'il le peut,
La rive fuit et le temps passe.
Voilà l'enfant au bord des cieux.

He saw himself

He saw himself quite often
Sitting at the foot of a hawthorn
Through whose leaves each roof-top
Sparkled, crowned with thorns.

Through tall harvest fields
A road went off on its own
To vanish near a lime tree
Behind the huge horizon.

A man he thought had his features
Because similarly made,
Approached, weary, beneath the beeches
Whose shadow covered the grass-glades.

And, worried sick, he wondered
Whether he was that man, the one
Who was endlessly setting off
Towards the night that didn't come.

The rowing boat

Not so far out, shrieks mummy.
And yet, already in his boat,
The child reaches the open sea
And won't hear a single word.

Waves laugh at his audacity,
Wind helps as much as he can,
Shoreline rushes away, time passes.
Now the child's where sea-sky began.

Ne voyez-vous rien, capitaine,
On dirait une barque folle?
Mais non, un albatros qui traîne
En rasant de très près les flots.

Ne vous lamentez plus, la mère,
C'est le chœur des sirènes bleues
Qui, avec tendresse, le mène
Au paradis des audacieux.

N'entendez-vous pas, quand la vague
Vient mourir sur le sable blond,
Cette voix qui, même un peu vague,
A votre seule voix répond?

Le voyageur

Il avait tant fait de voyages,
Couru tant de mers, de montagnes,
Rendu visite aux plus grands sages,
Vu tout ce que l'on pouvait voir,
Fait la guerre, non par devoir,
Mais pour mesurer son courage.
Alors, à quoi bon se leurrer?
Certainement l'éternité
Etait un abîme d'ennui
Et n'était pas faite pour lui.

Can you not see, captain,
What looks like a crazy boat?
No, just a slow albatross flying
Close to the waves, oh so close.

No more grieving, mother,
It's the blue sirens' choir
Which is tenderly leading him
To where the bold aspire.

Can you not hear, when the wave
Comes to die on blond sand,
That voice which, though rather vague,
Gives an answer only you'd understand?

The traveller

He had been on so many journeys,
Crossed so many seas,
Climbed so many mountains,
Had so many gurus put his mind at ease,
Seen all there was to see,
Fought in wars, not out of duty,
But to test his courage. So,
Why delude oneself? Come
Eternity there was no
Not even a slim
Chance it would be anything but
An abyss of boredom
For him.

Le débonnaire

Il est né avec ce cœur-là
Fait pour l'amour et pour la joie.

Il ne dit rien si on le bat,
Si on le couvre de crachats,
Si on le laisse à demi-mort,
Rien si on enfonce sa porte,
Rien non plus si on l'emprisonne.

Que pourrait-il dire d'ailleurs,
Lui qui n'entend, lui qui ne voit,
En ce monde, qu'avec son cœur
D'oiseau, d'enfant et de lilas?

Il s'assit

Les yeux sur les tarots,
Il leva la main droite.
Et, sans dire un seul mot,
Le champ de blé fondit.

Comme neige en avril,
Le ruisseau disparut,
Puis les bords du talus
Avec tous leurs pavots.

Après, ce fut le tour
Des lièvres, des oiseaux,
Du lac et du château
Avec ses quatre tours.

Seeing the good

He was born like that, kind-hearted,
Made for love and joy.

He says nothing if he's battered,
Spat upon, spattered
With slime and left half dead
In town.
Says nothing if his front door's bashed in,
Nothing even if he's sent down.

What could he say anyway,
As his heart, a kind heart,
A child's heart, only has room
For hearing the good
And seeing lilac in bloom?

He sat

With his eyes on the tarot cards,
He raised his hand, the right.
And without a single word,
The wheat-field melted from sight.

Like snow in April,
The stream lost its will
To stay, and the bank-slopes
Whisked their poppies away.

Next ones to vanish
Were birds, lake and hares,
Followed by the castle
With its four towers.

Alors, il n'y eut plus,
Si loin qu'il pût aller,
Qu'un plateau désolé
Sous ses pieds résolus.

Et, tranquille, il s'assit
Heureux au cœur d'un monde
Sans un pli, sans une ombre,
Un monde bien à lui.

Le mendiant

La mort riait, elle avait tort.
Il ne désirait, ce mendiant,
Ni pain, ni vin, ni pièce d'or,
Mais un lit à l'abri du vent,
Un lit dans n'importe quel coin
Où il pourrait dormir content.
Plus avare qu'une fermière,
La mort riait de sa misère
Comme si elle épargnait pour d'autres
Qui n'en avaient aucun besoin
Ses étroites et chaudes fosses
Et, lui montrant un peu de foin
Abandonné sur le chemin,
Lui fit un signe de la main
Et se perdit dans les lointains.

Then as far as he could go
Nothing else except
A desolate plateau
Under his resolute steps.

So, quietly, he sat down
Happy at the heart of a world
With no fold, no shadow,
His world, his very own.

The beggar

Death was laughing, was wrong to.
This beggar could do
Without bread,
Or wine, or riches, but wanted a bed
Sheltered from the wind, any-
Where he could sleep happy.
More tight-fisted than a farmer's wife,
Death laughed at his plight
As if saving for others (whose life
Had no need of them) her narrow
Warm ditches and, showing him
A little hay spilled
On the road,
Beckoned him
And disappeared from sight.

A force de le répéter

Qui sait, répétait-il, qui sait!
Tout est peut-être à effacer.
Qui sait, répétait-il, qui sait!
Il faudrait tout recommencer.
Qui sait, répétait-il, qui sait!
Peut-être est-il vain de prier?
Qui sait, répétait-il, qui sait!
Dieu même est à réinventer.

A force de le répéter,
Il crut qu'il en savait assez
Pour mettre le monde à ses pieds.
Et il ne se fit pas prier
Pour effacer, recommencer,
Réinventer, imaginer
Qu'il était au fond envoyé
Par les dieux, et même, qui sait!
Qu'il était ce dieu nouveau-né
Pour être cru et adoré.

Il disait oui

Il redisait oui de la tête,
    Oui, oui et encore oui
Sans le savoir telle une bête.

Et il ne savait pas non plus
    Comment cette façon
De faire lui était venue.

By dint of repeating it

Who knows, he repeated, who knows!
Everything may need obliterating.
Who knows, he repeated, who knows!
Everything would need reinstating.
Who knows, he repeated, who knows!
Perhaps there's no point in repenting?
Who knows, he repeated, who knows!
Even God needs reinventing.

By dint of repeating it
He thought his knowledge was complete
Enough to have the world at his feet.
And so he didn't need persuading
To rub everything out, to start again,
To reinvent,
To imagine he was sent
By the gods, and even, who knows!
That he was this new-born Lord
To be trusted and adored.

He said yes

He kept nodding his head
To say yes, yes and yes,
Not knowing what he'd said
Like a dumb beast.

And he didn't know either
How this way of doing things
Had come to him.

Il est vrai qu'il parlait aux meubles
    Luisant autour de lui.
Tous lui répondaient en aveugles.

Il est vrai que le balancier
    De l'horloge de chêne
Semblait sans fin l'interroger.

Et il redisait oui aux heures,
    Oui au monde, oui sans cesse
Même aux soucis, à la vieillesse
    Qui l'emportait sans heurt.

Regardez...

Regardez, dit-il, c'est un paquebot.
    Tous regardèrent
  Et dirent, c'est un paquebot.

Regardez mieux, dit-il, c'est un avion.
    Tous répondirent
  Que c'était bien là un avion.

Mais non, regardez mieux, c'est un nuage.
    Tous, ils admirent
  Qu'après tout, c'était un nuage.

Enfin, il s'écria: "Mais ce n'est rien!"
    Tous avouèrent
  Qu'en effet, ils ne voyaient rien.

It's true that he talked to the furniture
Shining around him.
Every piece responded blindly
As though blind.

It's true that the pendulum
Of the large oak clock
Seemed to pose him endless questions.

And he said yes to the hours,
Yes to the world, endlessly yes
Even to worries and old age
Which took him away with no stress.

Look...

Look, he said, it's a liner.
                They all looked
          And agreed it was a liner.

Look harder, he said, it's an aeroplane.
                They all replied
         Saying it was certainly a plane.

No, no, look harder still, it's a cloud.
                    All of them admired the fact
            That after all it was a cloud.

Eventually he shouted: "But there's nothing there!"
                They all confessed
          That actually they could see nothing.

Les choses

Les choses, disait-il, sont simples.
D'ailleurs, on ne voit pas comment
Elles pourraient être autrement.
La pomme est rouge; le bol, blanc,
Le couteau coupe les tartines
Sur la table de la cuisine.
Vienne le jour où l'on pourra
Parler tout simplement de l'homme
Comme l'on parle d'une pomme
Luisant sur la table de hêtre.
Quelle paix enfin sur la terre!

Dans la nuit

Il était seul avec la nuit,
    Mais seul aussi
   Avec sa propre nuit.
Et, dans sa nuit, pas plus d'étoiles
    Que dans la nuit
   Ecrasant la campagne.
Et il restait là, stupéfait,
Debout, derrière ses volets.

Il est vrai, il faut peu de chose
Pour déconcerter le destin.
La seule épine d'une rose
Peut dérouter la mort qui vient.

Things

Things, he'd say, are simple.
Besides, it's impossible to see
How they could be otherwise.
Apples are red; bowls white,
Bread-knives cut slices of bread
There on the kitchen table.
Come the day when folk will
Talk quite simply about man
Like they talk about apples
Shiny on a beechwood table-top.
What peace on earth at last!

In the night

He was alone with the night,
      But alone too
   With his own night.
And, in his night, no more stars
      Than in the night
   Crushing the countryside.
And he stayed standing there,
Shuttered in, dumbfounded.

Yet it doesn't take much
To confound fate.
A single rose thorn
Can throw approaching death off your track.

Il avait eu beau…

Il avait eu beau marcher,
Se presser, se reposer…
Toujours de nouveaux sentiers
Montaient le long des bouleaux,
Toujours une autre vallée
S'ouvrait entre les coteaux,
Toujours de nouveaux villages
Donnaient la main aux nuages
Et jamais, il le sentait,
Jamais il n'arriverait
Où son cœur le désirait.

La faim

Il ouvrit sa vieille armoire,
Et il en tomba du pain,
Puis, il tira le tiroir
Et il aperçut du vin.

Comment croire à ce miracle!
Le temps de tendre la main,
Il revoyait son armoire
Vide et vide le tiroir.

Comment pour mieux se moquer
Encor de son pauvre sort,
Le soleil semait de l'or
A foison sur le plancher.

In vain…

Despite all his walking,
Hurrying, then resting…
New paths kept stalking
Up past the birches,
Another valley would open out
Between the hill slopes,
Fresh villages would sprout
Houses and churches
And their handful of clouds,
Yet never, he could sense it,
Never would he arrive,
However much he hoped,
Where he'd be fully alive.

Hunger

He opened his old cupboard
And out fell some bread,
Then he gave the drawer a tug
And caught sight of wine.

A miracle of plenty!
But, stretching out a hand,
He saw his cupboard empty
And the drawer as well.

How could the sun, to mock
Him for his sad fate even more,
How could the sun sow gold
So abundantly on the floor?

Et l'araignée de la faim
Retissait dans son cerveau
Le plus cruel des réseaux
Machinés par le destin.

Que toute une allée…

Que toute une allée de statues
Puisse naître sur le passage
   D'une femme nue,
Voilà qui effrayait les sages.

Mais que l'on déclenche une guerre
Pour un motif aussi futile
   Qu'une clé de ville,
Cela ne les dérangeait guère.

Mon Dieu! que l'on fait bon marché
   De la vie d'un homme
Pour se disputer une pomme

Et qu'il faut une forte lampe
   Pour nous dénicher
Même sur une nappe blanche

Ne fût-ce qu'un grain de bonté!

And the spider called hunger
Re-spin in his upper storey
The cruellest of webs
Devised by destiny.

That a whole line...

That a whole line of statues
Could turn out to peruse
A naked woman walking by
Was enough to give the councillors a fright.

But when a war was waged
Over such a trifling affair
As the key to a town-gate
They hardly turned a hair.

Good heavens! that a man's life could
    Count for so little
In a dispute over an apple

And a strong torch be needed
    For us to spot
Even on a white tablecloth

    A single seed of goodness!

L'affamé

Il avait toujours faim,
Faim d'amour, faim d'espace,
Faim de la vie qui passe,
Faim rude qu'à la fin
Rien ne pouvait combler,
Faim toujours assoiffée
D'on ne sait quelle grâce
Qui l'aurait délivré
Enfin de son angoisse.

Ce petit rien

Un pêcheur immobile,
Des arbres alignés
Près du courant tranquille,
Des branches sur le ciel,
De longs vols d'hirondelles,
Une grange éloignée
Et, comme un faible écho
Montant des profondeurs,
L'inlassable rumeur
De l'eau dans les roseaux.

Et il se demandait:
"Mais que peut-il manquer
A ce site parfait?"
Sans jamais deviner
Ce que pouvait enfin
Etre ce grain de blé
Qui devait le combler.

The hungry man

He was always hungry,
Hungry for love, hungry for space,
Hungry for life that's passing.
A stark hunger that finally
Nothing could fill,
A hunger always thirsting
For some sort of grace
That might deliver him
At last from his anguish.

A little something

A motionless angler,
A line of trees
By the gentle current,
Branches against the sky,
Long flights of swallows,
A distant barn
And, like a feeble echo
Rising from the depths,
The tireless murmur
Of water in the reeds.

And he asked himself:
"What is it that's missing
In this perfect place?"
Without ever guessing
What the grain of wheat
Could be that would
Finally fulfil him.

L'homme et la mort

La mort parlait avec sa voix,
S'ébattait dans son corps,
Bouclait dans ses cheveux,
Peignait avec ses doigts,
Souriait dans ses yeux,
Et, quelquefois, la nuit,
Lui faisait entrevoir
La paix finale dans le noir
Avec tant de détails exquis
Qu'elle lui faisait, à l'aurore,
Regretter de n'être pas mort.

L'innocent du village

Il ne disait jamais rien,
Il n'entendait jamais rien,
Il ne lisait jamais rien,
Il n'écrivait jamais rien,
Ne pensait jamais à rien,
Bref, ne s'occupait de rien.
Il ne faisait que chanter
Des jours et des mois entiers
Et aller se promener
Dans le vent en liberté,
Et personne n'était plus sage.
C'était l'innocent du village.

The man and death

Death spoke with his voice,
Struggled in his body,
Curled in his hair,
Combed with his fingers,
Smiled in his eyes,
And, sometimes, at night,
Let him glimpse
Final peace in the dark
With so many exquisite details
That she made him, at dawn,
Regret he wasn't dead.

The village innocent

He never said anything,
He never grasped anything,
He never read anything,
He never wrote anything,
Never thought of anything,
In short, never took anything on.
All he did was sing
For days and months on end
And go off on walks
In the wind, free,
And no one was wiser.
He was the village innocent.

L'artiste

Mais pourquoi brûler un artiste?
        Répétait-il.
Nous avons trop besoin de bois
        Pour nos convois
        Et nos machines
   Pour l'employer aussi
      Mal à dessein.
Et on le regardait, sceptique...
       Pourquoi, ma foi
  En faire des martyrs?
      Ajoutait-il.
       Vous savez bien
Que presque tous meurent de faim.

Il aimait caresser

Il aimait caresser la lune,
La faire obéir mieux qu'un chien.
Il enfermait sans peine aucune
Le ciel tout entier dans la main
Et regardait, le soir, dans l'ombre,
Son cœur faire le tour du monde.
Mais il pleurait comme un enfant
Dès qu'on lui parlait de sa mère
Qui, pour le faire aussi puissant,
Etait morte dans la misère.

The artist

But why burn an artist alive?
              He kept repeating.
We've too great a need of wood
            For our wide loads,
                Our coffins and machines
   To want to use it so
                Ill-advisedly on purpose.
And people looked at him, sceptically...
            Why on earth
    Make martyrs of them?
            He would add.
               You know perfectly well
That almost everyone dies of hunger.

He loved stroking

He loved stroking the moon,
Making her obey better than a dog. And
With no trouble at all he'd soon
Have the whole sky in his hand.
He'd watch, as evening shades unfurled,
His heart travel right round the world.
But he'd weep like a child whenever
People mentioned his mother
Who, to make him as powerful as he
Now was, had died in poverty.

C'était si simple

Il écouta, comme il le faisait chaque soir,
    Le seau grincer en remontant du puits
Dans son jardin où les groseilliers étaient noirs
        De fruits.

    Ainsi que le balancier d'une horloge,
    Une étoile jaune allait et venait
        Dans le feuillage d'un cyprès.

    Des gens passaient. Leurs traînantes paroles
        S'emmêlaient un instant,
    Puis se perdaient comme des feuilles folles.

C'était si simple, si naturel tout cela
    Que jamais il ne s'était demandé
Si un jour viendrait où il ne serait plus là
        Pour les regarder.

Le tas de cendres

Etait-ce comme il le disait
A tous ceux qui voulaient l'entendre
La main subtile du destin
Qui répandait ce tas de cendres?

Il prétendait y déchiffrer
Même la mort si déguisée
Que, seul, il pouvait arriver
Quelquefois à la démasquer.

It was so simple

He listened, as he did every night,
To the bucket squeaking as it came up and out
            Of the well
In his garden where the blackcurrant bushes were quite
            Black with fruit.

    Like the pendulum of a clock,
    A yellow star swung to and fro
    Behind the foliage of a cypress.

    People passed. Their drawled words
            Intermingled a moment,
    Then got carried away like whirled leaves.

    It was so simple, things were so natural
        That he had never wondered
        Whether a day would come
    When he would no longer be there
            To see them.

The pile of ash

Was it like he said it would be
To all who wanted to hear him
That the discerning hand of destiny
Was spreading this heap of ash?

He claimed he could even make out
Death under her great disguise
And, alone, he could contrive
Sometimes to unmask her.

Cela n'allait pas sans erreur
Ni même sans extravagance,
La mort elle-même n'étant
Souvent qu'un petit tas de cendres
A la merci du premier vent.

Il chercha Dieu

Il chercha Dieu sur terre,
Le chercha dans la mer,

La lune, Vénus, Mars,
Le soleil, les étoiles,

Le chercha, étonné
De ne pas le trouver,

Sans jamais deviner
Que Dieu se confondait

Avec ce qu'il avait
De plus clair, de meilleur

En lui au fond du cœur.

He wasn't always far-seeing
Enough, sometimes he was just
Wildly wrong, death herself being
Often no more than a little heap of cinders
At the mercy of the first wind's gusts.

He searched for God

He searched for God on earth
He searched for him in the sea,

On the moon, on Venus, on Mars,
On the sun and the other stars,

Searched for him, was surprised
When he didn't find him,

And never even surmised
That God was within,

So here already, being
The brightest and best part

At the bottom of his heart.

L'animal

L'animal enchaîné cria.
On répondit du fond du bois.

Cependant, il ne vit personne
Marcher dans les feuilles d'automne.

L'animal cria de nouveau,
Un cri profond comme un sanglot.

Mais au loin, la voix s'était tue,
Enchaînée, eût-on dit, aux nues.

Et tout rentra dans un silence
Plus menaçant, plus sourd, plus dense.

Ils réclamaient

Ils réclamaient du pain,
Ils réclamaient des fruits.
On leur fit des usines
Ronflantes de machines
Et l'on mit dans leurs mains
Des bêches, des marteaux,
Des haches, des couteaux
Et même des fusils.

Et comme ils réclamaient,
Etonnants de candeur,
Ne fût-ce, dans la paix,
Qu'un semblant de bonheur,
On leur parla d'un Dieu
Cloué en croix pour eux.

The animal

The chained-up animal let out a yelp.
An answer came from deep in the wood.

And yet there was no one to be seen
Walking along through the autumn leaves.

The poor creature let out another yelp,
Deep-throated as a sob, for help.

But in the distance, the voice had died,
Chained, as it were, to a cloud's side.

And everything fell back into a silence
– More threatening, duller, more intense.

They were appealing

They appealed for bread,
They appealed for fruit.
They were given factories
Roaring with machines to suit
And they were provided
With spades, with hammers,
With axes, with knives
And even with guns.

And as they were appealing,
So candidly, surprisingly so,
For some sort of a feeling
Of happiness, in peace that would go
With everything, they were told,
Make no mistake, about a God
Nailed to a cross for their sake.

Il viendra

"Vous verrez", dit-il, "il viendra,
Celui qui est meilleur que moi."
Et le jour même de sa mort,
L'homme arriva plus simple encor
Et plus enclin à pardonner
Qu'on eût osé l'imaginer.
Mais à son tour, il répéta:
"Vous verrez, un jour, il viendra,
Celui qui est meilleur que moi."

Voici deux mille ans
Qu'en ce monde en feu, on l'attend.

He will come

"He's coming," he said, "you'll see,
The one who's better than me."
And the very day of his death,
The man, a simpler one, arrived,
One more inclined to forgive
Than anyone would have believed.
But he, with a fresh intake of breath,
Said: "He'll come one day, you'll see,
The one who's better than me."

It's been a good two thousand year
We've been waiting for him here
In this world that's on fire.

Biographical Notes

MAURICE CARÊME was born on 12 May 1899 in Wavre, a small town in Brabant-Wallon, Belgium, where his father Joseph was a painter and decorator and his mother, Henriette Art, ran a small grocery shop cum general store. One of his grandfathers sold goods from a gypsy caravan. His elder sister, born in 1898, only lived a day, his other sister, Germaine, was born in 1901; his younger brothers, Georges and Marcel, were born in 1904 and 1907 but Marcel only lived for eight months. Maurice had a very happy country childhood, which he often brought back to life in his poems. His first ones, written in 1914, were inspired by Bertha Detry, his childhood girlfriend. In the same year he won a scholarship to a teacher training college, the Ecole Normale de Tirlemont. Julien Kuypers was the teacher who encouraged him to write and introduced him to contemporary poetry.

In 1918 he left Wavre to become a primary school teacher in Brussels and in 1924 married Andrée Gobron, a fellow teacher (Caprine in his poems). The Brabant-style house he had built in Avenue Nellie Melba, is where they lived from 1933. It was known as 'la Maison Blanche' and became the seat of the Fondation Maurice Carême in 1975 and the Musée Maurice Carême on his death in 1978. He was 78.

He gave up teaching to write full-time in 1943. Author of some ninety books, novels, short stories, fables and essays, as well as poems, he published a collection of poems nearly every year from 1947 until 1975. *Mère* (1935) won the Prix Triennal de Poésie and *La maison blanche* (1949) the Prix de l'Académie Française. Where *Chansons pour Caprine* (1930) reflected quite a painful married life, his love poems were more discreet in *Femme* (1946) and, when inspired by Jeannine Burny, full of youthful vigour in *La bien-aimée* (1965). In Paris in 1972 he was elected "Prince des poètes" to succeed Jean Cocteau. He won numerous other prizes in Belgium and abroad, including one for his translation of Flemish poets. Even as a very weak 78 year old, he worked till the very last minute of his final afternoon, 13 January 1978.

Défier le destin appeared in 1987 and includes a selection of the poems he felt were finished. He had asked Jeannine (his friend and assistant since 1943 and now the President of the Fondation) to arrange the poems she was sure he had finished and for the cover of this collection she called on their friend, the artist Paul Delvaux. A subsequent collection, rather darker in tone, *De plus loin que la nuit*, appeared in 1992, and after a collection for the Gallimard Jeunesse series, *L'oiseleur et autres poèmes*, (2003), another, *Et puis après*, in 2004, and yet another *Être ou ne pas être* in 2008.

CHRISTOPHER PILLING was born in Birmingham and taught French and P.E on the Wirral, in a Quaker boarding school and a large Comprehensive in Yorkshire before moving to Keswick, Cumbria, where he taught French, German and Latin.

He was a prize-winner in the National Poetry Competition and has published nine collections of his own poetry, as well as translations of poems by Tristan Corbière (a Book of the Year for the *Sunday Telegraph* and the World Service of the BBC in 1995), Max Jacob and Lucien Becker (a PBS Recommended Translation in 2004). He has also written a number of plays.

With William Scammell, he founded a Cumbrian Poets' workshop which has run for thirty years, and has seen two of his plays performed at Theatre by the Lake in Keswick.

In 2006, Christopher Pilling won first prize in the John Dryden Translation Competition, one of the UK's most prestigious translation awards.

MARTIN SORRELL is Emeritus Professor of French and Literary Translation at the University of Exeter. He has published extensively. Among his books are *Elles: A Bilingual Anthology of French Poetry by Women* (1995) and, in Oxford University Press's 'World Classics' series, *Paul Verlaine: Selected Poems* (1999), *Arthur Rimbaud: Collected Poems* (2001) and *Frederico Garcia Lorca: Selected Poems* (2007).

Martin Sorrell has also written radio plays and stories for the BBC. He has won two translation prizes and his most recent radio play received a national award.

Also available in the Arc Publications
'VISIBLE POETS' SERIES
(Series Editor: Jean Boase-Beier)

No. 1
MIKLÓS RADNÓTI (Hungary)
Camp Notebook
TRANSLATED BY FRANCIS JONES
INTRODUCED BY GEORGE SZIRTES

No. 2
BARTOLO CATTAFI (Italy)
Anthracite
TRANSLATED BY BRIAN COLE
INTRODUCED BY PETER DALE
(Poetry Book Society Recommended Translation)

No. 3
MICHAEL STRUNGE (Denmark)
A Virgin from a Chilly Decade
TRANSLATED BY BENTE ELSWORTH
INTRODUCED BY JOHN FLETCHER

No. 4
TADEUSZ RÓZEWICZ (Poland)
recycling
TRANSLATED BY BARBARA BOGOCZEK (PLEBANEK) & TONY HOWARD
INTRODUCED BY ADAM CZERNIAWSKI

No. 5
CLAUDE DE BURINE (France)
Words Have Frozen Over
TRANSLATED BY MARTIN SORRELL
INTRODUCED BY SUSAN WICKS

No. 6
CEVAT ÇAPAN (Turkey)
Where Are You, Susie Petschek?
TRANSLATED BY CEVAT ÇAPAN & MICHAEL HULSE
INTRODUCED BY A. S. BYATT

No. 7
JEAN CASSOU (France)
33 Sonnets of the Resistance
WITH AN ORIGINAL INTRODUCTION BY LOUIS ARAGON
TRANSLATED BY TIMOTHY ADÈS
INTRODUCED BY ALISTAIR ELLIOT

No. 8
ARJEN DUINKER (Holland)
The Sublime Song of a Maybe
TRANSLATED BY WILLEM GROENEWEGEN
INTRODUCED BY JEFFREY WAINWRIGHT

No. 9
MILA HAUGOVÁ (Slovakia)
Scent of the Unseen
TRANSLATED BY JAMES & VIERA SUTHERLAND-SMITH
INTRODUCED BY FIONA SAMPSON

No. 10
ERNST MEISTER (Germany)
Between Nothing and Nothing
TRANSLATED BY JEAN BOASE-BEIER
INTRODUCED BY JOHN HARTLEY WILLIAMS

No. 11
YANNIS KONDOS (Greece)
Absurd Athlete
TRANSLATED BY DAVID CONNOLLY
INTRODUCED BY DAVID CONSTANTINE

No. 12
BEJAN MATUR (Turkey)
In the Temple of a Patient God
TRANSLATED BY RUTH CHRISTIE
INTRODUCED BY MAUREEN FREELY

No. 13
GABRIEL FERRATER (Catalonia / Spain)
Women and Days
TRANSLATED BY ARTHUR TERRY
INTRODUCED BY SEAMUS HEANEY

No. 14
INNA LISNIANSKAYA (Russia)
Far from Sodom
TRANSLATED BY DANIEL WEISSBORT
INTRODUCED BY ELAINE FEINSTEIN

No. 15
SABINE LANGE (Germany)
The Fishermen Sleep
TRANSLATED BY JENNY WILLIAMS
INTRODUCED BY MARY O'DONNELL

No. 16
TAKAHASHI MUTSUO (Japan)
We of Zipangu
TRANSLATED BY JAMES KIRKUP & TAMAKI MAKOTO
INTRODUCED BY GLYN PURSGLOVE

No. 17
JURIS KRONBERGS (Latvia)
Wolf One-Eye
TRANSLATED BY MARA ROZITIS
INTRODUCED BY JAAN KAPLINSKI

No. 18
REMCO CAMPERT (Holland)
I Dreamed in the Cities at Night
TRANSLATED BY DONALD GARDNER
INTRODUCED BY PAUL VINCENT

No. 19
DOROTHEA ROSA HERLIANY (Indonesia)
Kill the Radio
TRANSLATED BY HARRY AVELING
INTRODUCED BY LINDA FRANCE

No. 20
SOLEIMAN ADEL GUÉMAR (Algeria)
State of Emergency
TRANSLATED BY TOM CHEESMAN & JOHN GOODBY
INTRODUCED BY LISA APPIGNANESI

No. 21
ELI TOLARETXIPI (Basque)
Still Life with Loops
TRANSLATED BY PHILIP JENKINS
INTRODUCED BY ROBERT CRAWFORD

No. 22
FERNANDO KOFMAN (Argentina)
The Flights of Zarza
TRANSLATED BY IAN TAYLOR
INTRODUCED BY ANDREW GRAHAM YOOLL

No. 23
LARISSA MILLER (Russia)
Guests of Eternity
TRANSLATED BY RICHARD MCKANE
INTRODUCED BY SASHA DUGDALE

No. 24
ANISE KOLTZ (Luxembourg)
At the Edge of Night
TRANSLATED BY ANNE-MARIE GLASHEEN
INTRODUCED BY CAROLINE PRICE